Library of
Davidson College

THE HUMAN BODY
AND
THE LAW

Legal Almanac Series No. 76

THE HUMAN BODY AND THE LAW
LEGAL & ETHICAL CONSIDERATIONS IN HUMAN EXPERIMENTATION

by Charlotte L. Levy

1975 OCEANA PUBLICATIONS, INC.
Dobbs Ferry, New York

344.73
L668h

This is the seventy-sixth in a series of LEGAL ALMANACS which bring you the law on various subjects in nontechnical language. These books do not take the place of your attorney's advice, but they can introduce you to your legal rights and responsibilities.

Library of Congress Cataloging in Publication Data

Levy, Charlotte L
    The human body and the law.

    (Legal almanac series ; no. 76)
    Includes index.
    1. Medicine, Experimental--Law and legislation--United States. I. Title. [DNLM: 1. Ethics, medical. 2. Human experimentation. 3. Jurisprudence. W20.5 L668h]
KF3827.M38L48   344'.73'041   75-14041
ISBN 0-379-11101-2

© Copyright 1975 by Oceana Publications, Inc.

Manufactured in the United States of America

82-7161

TABLE OF CONTENTS

Introduction.	vii
Chapter 1 WHAT IS HUMAN EXPERIMENTATION?. . .	1
Documented Cases of Human Experimentation . . .	2
Chapter 2 PHILOSOPHICAL AND ETHICAL CONSIDERATIONS	6
Persons Lacking Understanding	9
Persons Lacking Freedom of Choice.	10
Conclusions.	14
Chapter 3 LEGAL CONSIDERATIONS.	15
Introduction.	15
General	16
Common Law	17
Tort Law.	19
Contract Law	23
Conclusion	25
Statutory Law.	26
Criminal Liability.	28
Administrative Law	28
Conclusion	30
Chapter 4 STERILIZATION	32
Compulsory Sterilization.	33
Voluntary Sterilization.	37
Criminal Liability.	42
Civil Liability.	43
Conclusion	44
Chapter 5 FETAL EXPERIMENTATION.	45
Philosophical History	45
Legal History.	46
Research Perspectives.	47
The Legal Response	48

Chapter 6 TRANSPLANTATION.	51
Transplantation as Experimentation	51
Legal Questions	52
Historical Legal Background.	53
Live Donors.	54
Minors and Incompetents	55
Cadaver Donors	56
Death.	57
Recipients.	59
Physician's Liability for Transplant Experimentation.	61
Chapter 7 THE UNIFORM ANATOMICAL GIFT ACT . .	63
The Pre-U.A.G.A. Legal Condition	63
State Adoption of the U.A.G.A.	64
Purposes of the U.A.G.A.	65
Unanswered Questions	66
Conclusion ·	67
Chapter 8 PSYCHOLOGICAL EXPERIMENTATION . . .	68
Experimental Nature of Somatic Behavior Control Therapy.	70
Legal Considerations.	71
Legal Consent	73
Psychopharmacology	75
Shock Therapy.	75
Psychosurgery.	76
Conclusion	77
Appendix A EUGENIC STERILIZATION STATUTES . . .	78
Appendix B CONNECTICUT GENERAL STATUTES §17-19	79
Appendix C STATE STATUTES PROHIBITING OR LIMITING FETAL EXPERIMENTATION.	80
Appendix D MASSACHUSETTS GENERAL LAWS, Ch.112 § 12 J.	81
Appendix E UNIFORM ANATOMICAL GIFT ACT	83

Appendix F	UNIFORM DONOR CARD.	87
Appendix G	NATIONAL RESEARCH SERVICE AWARD ACT OF 1974	88

Table of Cases 105

Index 107

INTRODUCTION

The purpose of this volume is to acquaint the reader with some of the ethical, medical, and legal considerations involved in human experimentation.

The problem is one that is quickly becoming one of grave concern to our society, as was concluded at a forum of the National Academy of Sciences, held in February, 1975, at which prominent lawyers, doctors, scientists, and academicians contributed significantly to the discussion. As reported in the New York Times of February 23, 1975, "complex" issues, such as the following were considered: (1) weighing the integrity of the individual's rights against society's gain when a volunteer risks his health in an experiment designed to acquire knowledge, not necessarily to directly benefit the volunteer; (2) determining how informed is informed consent when researchers detail the aims of an experiment but confront unknown hazards in carrying it on; (3) deciding who, if anyone, can substitute for the fetus or child in granting informed consent when their cells and other materials are crucial for research that seeks to solve the mysteries of aging and diseases that afflict adults; (4) whether informed consent can be truly obtained without fear or coercion from the poor, prisoners, military personnel, and other captive groups. All of these questions are explored, certainly, without definitive answers, in this Almanac.

In the first chapter we shall look at some documented cases of human experimentation and shall then attempt to define the term, "human experimentation." Chapter 2 will present the ethical problems inherent in human experimentation. Chapter 3 will introduce the reader to the legal implications and possibilities for control of human experimentation.

Considering the subject of human experimentation from its general to its particular aspects, we shall then examine several specific topics that lend themselves to a discussion of human experimentation. The topics that will be discussed are (1) sterilization, (2) fetal experimentation, (3) transplantation and the Uniform Anatomical Gift Act, and (4) psychological experimentation.

The materials in the appendices include examples of legislation dealing with human experimentation and lists of state statutes regulating fetal experimentation and sterilization. These appended materials will be referred to from time to time in the text.

Chapter 1

WHAT IS HUMAN EXPERIMENTATION?

According to a <u>New York Times</u> article published February 6, 1975, "$37,500 IS AWARDED FOR EACH SURVIVOR OF SYPHILIS PROJECT." The newspaper account refers to the Tuskegee, Alabama Syphilis Experiment in which 600 black males participated.

The forty-year-old study began in 1932. Its purpose was to determine the long-term effects of syphilis on untreated victims of the disease. Three hundred ninety-nine black men were left untreated and uninformed of the nature of their illness. Two hundred one additional men did not have syphilis but participated in the experiment as a nonsyphilitic control group. Eighty-five per cent of the 600 men had less than a sixth grade education. They were induced to join a social "lodge" by offers of free medicine (except for syphilis), free rides in limousines, cash payments of thirty-five dollars, inexpensive burials, and free hot meals on examination days. The experiment itself was sponsored by the federal government although the Milbank Memorial Fund, a private philanthropy, contributed monies for autopsies of the syphilis victims.

By 1936 cardiovascular disease resulting from central nervous system syphilis had infected a significant number of the untreated persons. By 1944 the mortality rate for the syphilis victims was double that of the control group. Even when penicillin became available after World War II, none of the men was treated and none was informed of the nature of his disease. By 1954 at least twenty-eight of the subjects had died as a direct result of untreated syphilis. By 1972, when Associated Press reporter Jean Heller broke the story, there were only seventy-four known survivors. All the known survivors were variously disabled, however, due to the untreated syphilis.

Some forty-one of the survivors of the experiment and a like number of heirs to those who failed to survive filed a class action suit against the federal government alleging total damages in the amount of $1.8 billion. Each plaintiff, including the 201 nonsyphilitic control group members, asked for $1.5 million in general damages and an additional $1.5 million under federal Tort Claims

Act. The recoverable total then would have been $3.0 million times 600 participants, or $1.8 billion. The out-of-court settlement was far less than the sum for which the suit was originally brought. Each syphilitic survivor received $37,500 and each living nonsyphilitic participant received $15,000 from the federal government. The estate of each deceased syphilitic participant received $15,000 and the estate of each nonsyphilitic participant received $5,000.

Whatever one may think of the adequacy of the out-of-court settlement, the Tuskegee syphilis experiment did at least receive some legal action. Very few documented cases of human experimentation even get to court. Most of the documented experiments that follow fall in that category.

Documented Cases of Human Experimentation

In 1966 a Harvard anesthesiologist, Henry K. Beecher, published an article in the New England Journal of Medicine. The subject of the article was the use of unethical or questionable ethical procedures in twenty-two experiments on human subjects. Although the biomedical research community appeared to be shocked, Robert Veatch, Ph.D., of the Hastings Institute, was able to testify before the United States Senate Subcommittee on Health of the Committee on Labor and Public Welfare in 1973, only seven years after the publication of the Beecher article, that the condition of ethically questionable experimentation was still widespread. He described the research designs of twelve human experimental studies that he selected from a collection of forty-three questionable experiments. The experiments reported by Veatch and Beecher were documented papers that had appeared in medical journals or had been presented at professional meetings. Brief accounts of some of those ethically questionable experiments follow.

Experiment 1. In an institute for mentally defective children in which a mild form of hepatitis was endemic, hepatitis was further induced artificially. The purpose of the study was to determine the period of infectivity of infectious hepatitis. The children were administered the hepatitis virus by injection or orally. Although the childrens' parents consented to the injections or the oral administration of the virus, they were not informed of the hazards involved.

Experiment 2. A group of servicemen were used in rheumatic fever experiments. It was known that rheumatic fever could be prevented by treating streptococcal respiratory infections with injections of penicillin. However, such treatment was withheld and placebos were given to the other servicemen. The treatment administered to each patient was based upon his military serial number. More men received penicillin than received the placebos. Two cases of acute rheumatic fever and one case of acute nephritis developed in the control patients. Those complications did not occur among those men who received the penicillin.

Experiment 3. Melanoma (a malignant tumor) was transplanted from a daughter to her mother. The purpose of the transplant was to gain a better understanding of cancer immunity in order to help in the treatment of cancer patients. The mother volunteered for the experiment and was considered to be informed. The daughter died the day following the transplantation of the tumor into her mother. The daughter's condition was considered terminal at the time the mother volunteered for the transplant. The primary implant was excised on the twenty-fourth day after it had been placed in the mother, who died from metastatic melanoma on the four hundred and fifty-first day after transplantation. The conclusive evidence was that the mother died from cancer caused by the transplanted tumor.

Experiment 4. In a study of immunity to cancer, twenty-two human subjects were injected with live cancer cells. The subjects were all hospitalized patients. They were told that they would be **receiving some cells. No mention was** made of the word "cancer."

Experiment 5. Twenty-four male subjects answered an advertisement for experimental subjects; they were to be paid two dollars per hour to participate in drug experiments. The purpose of the study was to determine the long-range personality, attitude, value, interest, and performance change in the experimental subjects. The twenty-four males received 200 micrograms of LSD, whereas the control group composed of twenty-four other subjects received amphetamines and 25 micrograms of LSD. The subjects were not informed of possible personality or other changes that could result from the experiments. Fifteen percent of the subjects had never before heard of LSD and another 73 percent had only casual knowledge of the drug.

Experiment 6. In order to test a newly developed dispenser for vaginal foam, 2,932 women, most of whom were medically indigent, agreed to use vaginal contraceptive foam as their only method of contraception. The women were recruited from five clinics and one physician's private practice. As a result of the use of this known unreliable method of birth control, there were ninety-four pregnancies for a pregnancy rate of 3.98 per hundred women-years of exposure.

Experiment 7. An experiment to study plasma renin levels in patients who had had both kidneys removed was conducted on ten patients who had had their kidneys removed only two weeks prior to the experiment. The ten patients were hospitalized for an eight-day period. On the third day of the experiment the subjects were clinically dehydrated. On another day measurements were taken after the patients had been standing quietly for two hours. In order for the patients to even accomplish this two hours of standing, most of them had to lean on a chest-high supporting table and had to be encouraged to continue to stand. Prior to that time serum samples were taken only when the patients were supine because of the severe hypotension and near fainting that developed in standing.

Experiment 8. In order to test the effectiveness of cromolyn sodium in blocking asthma attacks, nine children aged 11 1/2 to 16, all of whom suffered from asthma, were intentionally subjected to challenge doses of antigens that were known to produce asthmatic attacks. They were subject to a total of fifty-five antigen challenges. Twenty of these challenges were preceded by cromolyn sodium treatment. Each child experienced at least one "severe" reaction to the antigen challenges. And delayed asthmatic reactions occurred from six to twelve hours after the challenges in five of the nine children. Furthermore, although seven of the nine children required regular medication for their asthmatic conditions, this medication was withheld for a period of eighteen hours prior to the study.

The above examples of documented cases of human experimentation are shocking and infuse the two words - human experimentation - with a somber timbre. Is human experimentation always bad, ugly, frightening? What then is human experimentation?

Human experimentation may be defined as the use of human subjects in medical/scientific experiments that serve to advance medical science. If such a definition of human experimentation is too broad, it can be narrowed by honing in on possible interpretations of the definition. There are divergent opinions among medical professionals concerning the meaning of human experimentation. Some medical professionals argue that new drugs and therapeutic approaches that are tried daily in hospitals, clinics, and physicians' offices constitute human experimentation. Others say that novelty *alone* does not yield human experimentation.

Rather, these innovative practices are for the good of the patient and do not cause the patient harm. Instead of using innovation as the criterion for human experimentation, these medical professionals would suggest the extreme of pure scientific research on healthy subjects. However, a third more moderate interpretation which is probably accepted by a majority of medical personnel categorizes human experimentation as the use of insufficiently tested medical methods that the medical community has neither accepted nor rejected, on human subjects, the purpose of which is either one or both of the following: (1) to help the patient; (2) to advance medical science.

Chapter 2

PHILOSOPHICAL AND ETHICAL CONSIDERATIONS

Any definition that stipulates "the use of human subjects" or "the use . . . on human subjects" needs to be examined in terms of ethics. It seems at first glance that using human beings as research guinea pigs is an ethical dilemma of considerable magnitude. It sounds as though medical and/or scientific ethics are precluded when children are infected with hepatitis or subjected to antigen doses known to produce asthmatic attacks. Likewise one wonders about man's inhumanity to man when one envisions persons who have recently had both kidneys removed standing for two hours or hospitalized patients being injected with live cancer cells.

Indeed some people bristle at the very idea of experimenting with human beings and they are not willing to discuss it further. Other people believe that human experimentation is a necessary evil that can be justified in order to benefit medicine and science. Such strong reactions are often impulsive and lack thoughtful reflection. Before such absolute value judgments can be imposed it is necessary to consider the subject of human experimentation very carefully and to devote particular attention to the ethical principles involved in human experimentation. Sometimes fact situations that totally change the parameters of a given condition or situation present themselves. That is, there are occasions when situation ethics may apply. It is therefore advisable to consider each situation based upon its own facts. Fewer and fewer categorical imperatives apply given the increasing secularization of human existence and human experience.

Applying the situation ethics concept to human experimentation, let us assume that a possibility exists to cure a patient's fatal illness if he will submit to a procedure of an experimental nature. In this example we shall suppose that the ill subject is an adult who has been treated by a team of doctors with extremely sophisticated knowledge and skills, as well as the most technologically advanced equipment. Now since this person is terminally ill and treatment has been unavailing, premature death seems inevitable. Therefore one might venture that the person has nothing to lose, but surely something to gain by submitting to experiments as a human subject.

But surely the previous statement can easily be shredded word by word. For, the person often loses intangibles such as human dignity, privacy, freedom of movement, and so forth. And, of course, the chances of gain are on a sliding scale dependent upon infinite combinations of factors: the skill of the medical researchers, the state of experimentation at the point in time when the human becomes the subject of the experiment, the reversibility of the illness even if a cure were discovered, etc.

However, one could here include the fact that even if the immediate human subject does not benefit from the experiment, someone else will. The immediate subject will add to the corpus of medical/scientific knowledge, thereby benefiting existing society and future generations. Would this not be a good, an even great deed for mankind, were this chronically ill person to sacrifice himself for the benefit of contemporary and future society? Perhaps. Yet, in one of the simplest examples we are confronted with a multitude of ethical problems. The example is simple in that we have a terminally ill adult who has had the advantage of the most competent medical care. Even so, the inevitable conflicts arise. Why should this person give up his individual rights for the rest of mankind? What if he is unwilling to do so? What if he would rather die a dignified death in terms of retaining his corporeal privacy and mental tranquility? Who may tell him what he may or may not do? Or, in the event he is willing to participate in the experiment as a subject, what are the limits of the experiment and the experimenter and who shall set up and monitor these limits?

Let us now modify the example so that we are concerned with an adult who is perfectly healthy but who is to be the subject of an experiment. First of all, let us consider why a normal, healthy subject would be needed for experimentation. Although the subject himself is not seeking an immediate cure, the answer is fairly obvious. In order to determine the deleterious, innocuous, or benign effects of drugs or foreign substances when introduced into the human system, healthy subjects must be used. Or, persons of normal health are often needed to form a control group in various human experiments. But, you might ask, cannot animals be substituted in these instances to reach the desired results? Not always. For example, in the attempt to understand and control heart disease in the countries where the disease is prevalent, researchers have not been able to find any species of animal that independently develops coronary thrombosis as it exists in humans. Nor can coronary thrombosis, as it is known in humans, be induced in animal species. Hence, in order to determine hazardous quantities of particular substances in the human diet, one might suggest injections of cholesterol directly into the blood streams of persons with very low cholesterol levels. A control group would be set up and the persons in this group would ingest only polyunsaturated fats.

Absent inducements such as financial rewards, reduced sentences or freedom in the case of prisoners, a healthy subject would gain nothing from participating in an experiment as suggested above. Since the risk of loss would be great, however, it is difficult to imagine anyone submitting to such an experiment. The possible exception might be where the researcher himself becomes so intent upon proving his hypothesis--for example, massive injections of cholesterol do or do not cause heart attacks--that he himself is willing to become his own subject.

At any rate, once we remove the possibility of cure of the immediate subject, we approach a situation that, in its extreme form, may have nothing at all to do with benefiting mankind. If the advancement of medical science is given secondary importance or disregarded completely, then human experimentation can take on negative values. The less the pure research value of human experimentation can be balanced against advances to benefit mankind, the less tolerable human experimentation becomes. In fact, carried a step farther, human experimentation can be used to the detriment of mankind.

For instance, let us consider a situation wherein a group of healthy adults are subjected to various levels of radiation even though it is generally known that certain amounts of radiation are fatal. Let us assume that the purpose behind these experiments is to determine exactly how much radiation would be required to destroy an enemy population within a given period of time but simultaneously not be fatal to a neighboring nonenemy population. Putting aside the insuperable ethical problems posed by the destruction of a population by radiation warfare, there are problems inherent in using a healthy group of subjects when fatality is a known result. And even where the radiation dosage (number of rads) may not necessarily be fatal, the risk of harm is not likely to be ameliorated by the objective of being able to destroy an entire population. It is difficult to construe such an end as beneficial to mankind without perverting the meaning of mankind itself. The point then becomes that the ethical questions are complex, with each variable (health, terminal illness, etc.) figuring into the eventual equation that hopes to balance the interests of the individual with the interests of society.

As if the ethical problems concerning ill versus healthy adult research subjects were not complicated enough, special classes of persons need to be considered. We shall be considering special classes excluding legally defined adults of at least average intelligence who are able to comprehend the nature and possible consequences of a particular experiment.

The special classes of persons requiring special consideration vis-a-vis human experimentation may be divided into two broad categories: (1) persons lacking understanding; and (2) persons lacking freedom of choice. The first category includes minor children, feeble-minded and mentally ill persons, as well as some aged persons; the second category includes prisoners, socio-economically deprived persons, and addicted persons.

Persons Lacking Understanding

Children, the feeble-minded, the mentally ill, the aged, and others who would come under the heading of persons lacking understanding need a protective aegis from would-be human experimenters. For this group poses special considerations since its members are not in positions to completely understand the parameters of a given experiment. Therefore, even their voluntary participation in a human experiment becomes meaningless since they do not have the ability to give meaningful consent.

Who then, may give consent for such individuals? A parent, a legal guardian, the state? The question is not so difficult to answer if the experiment will directly benefit the individual concerned. In that situation, the interests of the individual and the interests of society coincide. However, if the interests conflict we have an ethical dilemma of new dimensions.

To pose the questions let us take a relatively simple example. Let us assume we are concerned with a healthy child as the subject of an experiment. Further, we shall assume that the child's situation is such that both parents are living and are concerned with the welfare of the child. But what if the healthy child has an identical twin who is dying because of kidney failure? Do the parents have the right to decide that the healthy child shall give one of its kidneys to its dying twin? In view of the results of current experimentations in which one identical twin seems to tolerate transplanted bone marrow of the other twin in the successful treatment of leukemia, one would be inclined to think that a kidney transplant between identical twins would most likely restore the afflicted twin since there is little chance of rejection of the tissue. And yet who has the right to demand the risk of harm that may accrue in the case of the healthy child? And what if the donor twin, who now has one kidney, is in an automobile accident in which his remaining kidney is punctured? Is such an occurrence at all foreseeable; if so, does it not also warrant some attention?

Or what if the parents are not confronted with such a genuinely unfortunate dilemma as in the case of the twins? What if the parents are simply greedy and are therefore willing to submit their children to experimentation that tests pharmaceuticals for children in return for high monetary compensation? May the parents subject their children to this kind of experimentation? Or are there philosophical considerations that might or should stop them?

Although we shall not consider the feeble-minded, mentally ill, and aged in detail, their special problems in relation to human experimentation should be noted. Here there are added psychological considerations if the feeble-minded or mentally ill have parents and the aged have children who would be responsible for deciding the roles of feeble-minded and other special persons in human experiments. There are often subconscious feelings of guilt, anger, embarrassment, and resentment by children or parents toward those for whom they are responsible. Therefore, one would question whether such feelings might interfere with deciding what may be in the best interests of the potential experimental subjects.

If parents or others legally responsible for children, the aged, etc. may not be in positions to consent to human experimentation for those toward whom they owe responsibility, what about allowing the state to decide the matter? The state's deciding matters of who shall become human subjects would cause many people to bristle and recoil in fear and anger. Permitting the state to decide such matters under current administrative apparatus and bureaucratic procedures may at best be a risky business. For the state is by necessity impersonal and its machinery so vast that a slight error might do irreparable harm to someone unable to defend his own rights. Thus if the state's involvement is not questionable from a philosophical viewpoint, it is certainly dubious from a practical point of view.

Persons Lacking Freedom of Choice

Since our purpose is not exclusively philosophical it would be pointless to explore free will versus determinism. Rather we shall begin with the dubious proposition that human beings are free to choose to act or not to act. Certainly, when we think of individuals making decisions to participate in or forego human experiments as the subjects thereof, we like to believe that their freedom to choose is as unrestricted as possible. It follows, then, that if an individual's ability to choose is obstructed in any appreciable manner, it becomes necessary to consider such individuals in a category separate from the mainstream of society. There are perhaps several subcategories of persons here. We shall consider three special classes of persons as examples of individuals whose freedom of choice is restricted.

Prisoners. We limit our definition of prisoners to those persons incarcerated in institutions of criminal correction. Prisoners have traditionally been recruited as "voluntary" healthy subjects of experiments. However, the voluntariness of their participation is suspect. What if the prisoners are induced to participate in the experiments by promises of reduced sentences, time off for good behavior, or simply additional prison privileges during their incarceration? We might also want to consider the more subtle pressure of alleviating boredom. The prospect of participating in an experiment may somewhat relieve the boredom of prison life by at least offering a change of scene and contacts with the nonprison environment. Even if the experiments are conducted within the prison facilities, the contact with the medical researchers as representational symbols of the outside world might suffice to produce a feeling of changed environment. Further we shall suppose that some prisoners honestly wish to redeem themselves on society's terms and thus see participation in experiments to benefit society as a means of assuaging the guilty verdict that society has rendered unto them. Or, we shall suppose that "volunteering" for such experiments might build the volunteer's self esteem or esteem of fellow prisoners. Prisoners' inducements and motives may vary considerably, and society may or may not deem such inducements and motives sufficient to disallow the use of prisoners for human experiments. The point is that the unique situation of prisoners must at least be considered.

Socio-economically Deprived Persons. In reviewing documented case studies of human experimentation, the fact that socio-economically deprived segments of society are disproportionately used in experiments becomes evident. Nor need we dig very far to seriously question whether or not these poor persons can be said to have voluntarily submitted to the experiments. But, let us begin by uncluttering our minds and assuming that these persons did volunteer for experimentation. If these persons volunteered with absolutely no strings attached, there are no ethical problems in terms of free will.

However, what if some welfare recipients were given the incentive to volunteer themselves as subjects in exchange for additional welfare funds? Or what about an upwardly mobile university student from an extremely poor family? Assume that the student has a full tuition scholarship but is having a difficult time covering other expenses. What if this student were offered a reasonable living allowance if he would volunteer as a subject for experimental research? Is the psychological inducement--to be able to live like most of the other students and be free from financial worries--enough an incentive to bring into question the student's freedom of choice?

For a more clearcut set of facts, which may nevertheless produce greater extremes in philosophical opinion, let us assume the following: A group of poor persons with nutritionally unsound high-starch diets is selected because of obesity problems. No one in the group has more than a fifth-grade education. Suppose a medical researcher concerned with obesity problems explains the hazards of continued obesity to them in terms that they can understand. He then proceeds to explain how their conditions can be improved by surgery that will remove part of their small intestines. He shows them "before and after" photographs of other persons who have undergone such operations. He glosses over the risks involved in an operation that has not gained widespread acceptance within the medical community. And perhaps most important, the researcher intends to sever more or less of the intestines of the subjects, depending upon the extent and duration of their obesity, than is recommended. He has explained this to the subjects, but in scientific terms no one fully understands.

The medical researcher is able to obtain the consent of these people. However, were these people able to give consent that was based upon freedom of choice? Or was the consent obtained through fraud or coercion? Some would say consent was given. Others would say it was not. And there might even be a third opinion ventured that such people should never or hardly ever be recruited as experimental subjects on the grounds that complicated factors such as unfamiliarity with medical procedures and subtle intimidation by the status of medical personnel restrict their freedom of choice.

At this point, another might retort that surely someone who

is merely lacking intellectual sophistication, but who has a normal level of intelligence, can be brought to a level of understanding in such matters. Assuming that the proposition is true, are medical researchers willing and have they the time to enlighten each person concerning present-day medical procedures?

Addicted Persons. There may be a question of classification of addicted persons. That is, are addicts those lacking freedom of choice or are they mentally ill persons lacking understanding? Let us deal with drug addicts, including alcoholics, and for the moment consider their compulsion to take drugs as a physical dependency over which they have little control, in the advanced stages of the disease. The fact is that the drug addict of normal intelligence is capable of understanding except perhaps during moments of stupor or hallucination or delirium. And yet, his compulsion for amphetamines, heroin, or alcohol may overpower his understanding so that his sphere of freedom of choice is severely circumscribed.

For example, most persons are aware that alcoholics have been able to sell their blood for a fee in the past. And the fee was used to buy more alcohol. The alcoholic's blood was subsequently sold to blood banks. Since this practice was mainly a commercial one, the alcoholics were not adequately screened for hepatitis and certainly most establishments didn't bother about the frequency with which the alcoholic was giving blood. And even if the question was perfunctorily asked, the alcoholic needed only to fill in the perhaps untruthful but necessary information. Such practices have in fact been more or less discontinued because there were problems of contaminated blood appearing in blood banks.

For the purpose of illustration, however, let us suppose that the practice hasn't entirely ended. Thus, a group of alcoholics has been recruited from the blood donors as subjects for an experiment. The only requirement is an already damaged liver. The researcher offers to keep the alcoholics in booze but they will have to remain within designated quarters for continuity of observation. What the researcher intends to do is to inject into their blood streams a chemical that he believes should stimulate regeneration of dead liver tissue. However, it is also possible that the chemical will upset the balance of other cells and thus cause cancer in the subjects. Assuming for a moment that the alcoholics are willing to give up the rituals and life style associated with the Bowery or Skid Row, or that they are not suspicious that they are really going to be "dried out," we shall suppose that some of them have accepted. We shall also assume that the procedure and risk of harm have been explained to the individuals and that they have signed consent forms. Now, has the subject truly consented of his own accord or has his overwhelming goal in life of drinking himself into oblivion so obscured his ability to think rationally that his freedom of choice can be said to be practically nonexistent?

Conclusions

When considering human experimentation, we learn that we are dealing with complex questions wherein many variables interface and many interests must be balanced. At either extreme of the philosophical spectrum is a priority. At one extreme is the Judeo-Christian ethic of the centrality and transcendent worth of the individual. At the other extreme is the supremacy and exultation of the ideal (e.g. state, knowledge, aesthetics, etc.). And at various points between the extremes lie potential balances. That is, at the less obsessional zones of the extremes, medical knowledge can be advanced without the degeneration of our widely held value that individual human life should receive priority.

We see that we are philosophically involved in two broad areas: (1) man's relationship toward his fellow man, and (2) man's relationship toward the state. Traditionally these philosophical areas have required rules and regulations. Therefore, after we have questioned ourselves about the various ethical problems involved in experimentation with human beings and have independently arrived at our own conclusions, it may be fruitful to examine a particular legal system to determine the present state of the law. After examining the current law we should then try to evaluate its applicability to the specific kinds of human experimentation (sterilization, transplantation, fetal research, etc.). We shall thus turn to the examination of the United States legal system and how the United States federal law and the various state laws attempt to control human experimentation.

Chapter 3

LEGAL CONSIDERATIONS

Introduction

Human experimentation is becoming increasingly newsworthy. On a global scale it is no longer confined to the pages of medical and scientific journals. One only needs to pick up newspapers from one country or another to find articles concerning human experimentation. "TEST TUBE BABY BORN IN BRITAIN CLAIMS DOCTOR," reads a British newspaper headline. (The Daily Telegraph (Final ed.), London, July 16, 1974, p.1.) Churches publicly opine that this is ethically acceptable or warn that caution must prevail because no one knows what may happen to test tube children. But for those persons interested in human experimentation from a legal point of view, there is a conspicuous absence of legal opinion in newspaper accounts.

The law has been slow to act in the area of human experimentation. This may be a source of chagrin in that one or two unfortunate accidents from human experimentation have resulted (e.g., Thalidomide babies). Similar accidents will force the law to step in. But, this situation is typical. That is to say, the law is a social science. It reacts very slowly to social needs. Since the law is a slow evolutionary science, it cannot even keep up with scientific medical progress that is revolutionary, much less outpace it. Unpalatable consequences are certain to ensue. But the law will eventually step in. For example, experiments at the University of Cincinnati College of Medicine for treating cancer patients with radiation led to a Senate investigation of the matter and to a Congressional bill, H.R. 7724 which originated in the House, sponsored by the House Committee on Interstate and Foreign Commerce, chaired by Rep. Paul Rogers and which was then referred to the Senate Committee on Labor and Public Welfare, chaired by Sen. Edward Kennedy. (See Appendix G for the text of H.R. 7724.) And yet, undesirable consequences may still be requisite before the law can react because the results of experimentation must first reveal their effects on society. For the law to react rigidly and prematurely might unduly obstruct the beneficial consequences of human experimentation.

To be sure, some systematic regulation of human experimentation is inevitable. But what form this regulation will take is more difficult to predict. In the paragraphs that follow we shall examine existing law applicable to human experimentation and perhaps try to extrapolate therefrom in order to ascertain possible future developments.

General

Before we can fully appreciate the legal problems inherent in human experimentation, we must grasp two fundamental aspects of the United States legal system. First, the legal system prevailing in the United States is basically a common law system. Let us, however, consider what we mean by the common law. Through popular usage, "common law" has come to be used in at least three different ways. First, common law refers to the English system of law in its entirety as well as legal systems, such as that of the United States, that are derived from it. Secondly, the term is applied to distinguish statutory law by legislative enactment from judge-made law by the operation of the courts. And finally, common law is sometimes used to distinguish courts of equity from courts of law.

When referring to the common law we shall mean the second definition of the common law, i.e., uncodified law that is based on judicial precedent. For simplification we shall refer to the common law as judge-made law. This means that theoretically each legal case is looked at anew and the judges render an order dependent upon the particular facts of the case. They are, however, guided by opinions previously rendered if the facts are the same or similar.

But this is only half the picture. It does not take a legal expert to advise us that there is a federal code, the United States Code, as well as state codes (or statutes), e.g. the Ohio Revised Code or Kentucky Revised Statutes. What then are these codes and statutes, if not written compilations of laws? They are in fact written laws. What has happened is that as the legislatures promulgated laws these were set down. What we have then is a legal system in which judge-made law and legislative law (or statutory law) run concurrently. The legislature issues laws that the judiciary interprets or construes. Even though our laws are becoming more and more codified and there are fewer strictly common law or judge-made principles extant, some do persist.

Moreover, in order to complete the legal framework of

human experimentation we need to know something about administrative law--generally a body of binding regulations developed by responsible agencies set up by statute or executive order. It is worth understanding the nuances distinguishing judge-made law, statutory law and administrative law, as well as their integral relationships in order to understand human experimentation in its legal context. And perhaps we shall even find ourselves asking whether one type of law or the other might be preferable for the basic regulation of human experimentation.

The second fundamental aspect of United States law that must be emphasized is that the United States Constitution leaves to the individual states the power to make laws governing human experimentation. This, of course, complicates our study of the current legal situation with respect to human experimentation, because we must look to the statutes of each state and to its judicial opinions. And we must do so under separate subheadings. That is, we cannot go to the index of a state's statutes, turn to the heading Human Experimentation, and expect to find our answers. We must show much more ingenuity and resourcefulness and look under a multitude of subcategories such as Sterilization, Organ Transplants, Malpractice, Physicians and Surgeons, etc.

At that point we may pull our hair and think it would be easier if a state's statutes concerning human experimentation were consolidated or at least indexed under the term. Undoubtedly. But, as we shall explore in somewhat greater detail, human experimentation as a legal entity has but recent roots, to be sure.

Well, you might say, let us get on with it and have the United States Congress make us some laws governing the whole question, then we won't have to drift about and guess. We must constantly keep in mind the fact that federal laws and regulations will only be applicable in limited instances, for example, where the federal government grants funds for medical research. Otherwise, the federal government's authority stops where the state government's authority begins. You may wonder about the efficacy of such a system when one is dealing with laws affecting human life. But, we must remember that the individual states also have the power to rescind capital punishment and they have the power to reinstitute it.

Common Law

Remember that we mean by the common law, judicial decisions or judge-made laws that are administered by the courts.

Now, you may be surprised to learn that actual litigated cases involving human experimentation are rare. Some of the reasons why few human experimentation lawsuits are brought include the following: (1) there is a great deal of expense, time, and energy involved in bringing a lawsuit; (2) subjects are often recruited from socio-economically deprived segments of the population and thus do not know their rights or have access to the powers that could help them defend their rights; (3) subjects are usually unaware of the necessary evidence they need to prosecute a claim; (4) terminally-ill subjects as well as those who are fatally injured do not live long enough to get into the courts; (5) members of the medical profession are not eager to testify against one another; and (6) most persons are simply hesitant to bring lawsuits generally. This paucity of case law concerning human experimentation is compounded by the fact that courts have not recently distinguished between human experimentation and malpractice suits.

The early Anglo-American cases seemed to be on the right track in considering experimentation apart from medical malpractice. The two earliest and most cited cases in any discussion of human experimentation are Slater v. Baker (2 Wils. (K.B.) 359, 95 Eng. Rep. 860 (1767)) and Carpenter v. Blake (60 Barb. (N.Y.) 488, rev'd on other grounds, 50 N.Y. 696 (1872)).

In the Slater case, a famous London surgeon tried to refracture the patient's improperly healed leg in order to straighten it. The surgeon used a novel bone breaking device without the patient's consent. The court explicitly disapproved of experimentation in the case and laid down the rule that if a physician departs from an established system of treatment he does so at his own peril.

The leading American decision, the Carpenter case, was not a true case of experimentation, but the court did discuss the issue. In that case, a surgeon failed to inform the patient concerning the care of a dislocated elbow after it had been reset. The Carpenter case limited liability for experimentation to cases in which an experimental procedure is used even though there are existing methods of treatment.

However, since these early cases the courts have hopelessly muddled the issues of experimentation and malpractice. They have designated all departures from approved medical practice as experimentation whether or not experimentation was involved. In addition, unorthodox medical treatment, often bordering on quackery, has been included under the penumbra of "experimentation." The crux of the confusion of the courts has been the failure to separate experimentation from a physician's lack of skill and knowledge possessed by other practitioners in the community and/or his failure to apply such skill and knowledge as would be reasonably expected under the circumstances.

Likewise, common law doctrines traditionally associated with medical malpractice suits are generally applied in judicial decisions concerning human experimentation. Some of the common law causes of action that can be applied to cases of human experimentation will be discussed below. But first, it may be helpful to mention that an experimenter might be criminally liable as well as civilly liable. However, since criminal law in the United States is primarily statutory, we shall presently consider only the common law tort and contract theories of civil liability in the paragraphs that follow. And since most common law claims are likely to arise under tort theories (they are more plentiful in the breach of a doctor-patient relationship), we shall first consider tort law and its primary defense, consent. Secondly, we shall consider applicable contract law.

Tort Law

A tort is a civil wrong that results in the injury of another and that entitles the injured party to claim damages. "Civil" is used to distinguish the wrong from a criminal wrongdoing. Torts that could result from human experimentation follow.

Negligence. Negligence may be defined as (1) not doing something that should be done, or (2) doing something that should not be done at all, or (3) doing something that should be done differently. Alternately, negligence may be defined as the failure to use a reasonable standard of care where a duty of care exists. Negligence becomes an actionable tort if it results in the injury of another. Negligence is the most common cause of action brought by patients against medical professionals in malpractice suits. Negligence is often easy to prove in a malpractice suit since physicians are held to a higher standard of care than that of the ordinary reasonable man. Physicians are expected to have the competence to reasonably foresee likely consequences of their professional acts.

In a typical malpractice suit for negligence, the plaintiff (injured party) must prove he was damaged by the physician. There is, however, an exception to his necessity for proving damages. This specific kind of negligence is called res ipsa loquitur and retains its Latin meaning of "the thing speaks for itself." In a res ipsa situation, a given set of facts is so supportive of the defendant's negligence, that the burden of proof shifts to the defendant and it is he who must prove that his negligence did not result in the plaintiff's injury.

By way of illustration, consider that a post mortem reveals that a person who recently underwent minor abdominal surgery died of internal hemorrhaging. It is further revealed that the internal bleeding was caused by the surgeon's scalpel which lodged itself in the small intestine and which had lacerated the stomach and small intestine. In such a case it is obvious that the surgeon or one of his assistants was extremely negligent. Thus the burden would be on the members of the surgical team to prove they were not negligent.

Assault and Battery. The terms assault and battery are popularly used together. But technically, an assault is a mere attempt or threat to use force upon the person of another. And a battery is technically a completed assault whereby actual force is applied to the person of another. Thus every battery contains an assault, although an assault need not result in a battery. Both assault and assault and battery are actionable as torts.

Fraud. The tortious action of fraud arises when someone makes a false representation of fact that he knows to be false. In addition, the person making the false representation must intend that the false representation be acted upon. Finally, the plaintiff must have acted upon the false misrepresentation and been damaged or injured thereby. For example, a physician might proclaim that he has perfected a sterilization operation that is 100 percent reversible. The procedure has not been approved by the medical profession as a safe operation and is thus experimental. Furthermore, the operating physician himself does not even believe this statement that the operation is 100 percent reversible. Therefore if persons underwent the operation only to subsequently discover that they are irrevocably sterile, they might base claims on the tort theory of fraud.

Invasion of Privacy. An action for invasion of privacy could theoretically lie on at least two grounds: (1) intrusion and (2) public disclosure of private facts.

Intrusion may consist of one person encroaching upon another's physical solitude or seclusion. A possible example of intrusion in relation to medical malpractice or human experimentation would be a surgeon summoning large audiences of medical school students and candidates for Ph.D's in physiology to view a particular operative procedure if the surgeon had not obtained the patient's prior consent.

The public disclosure of private facts is self-explanatory as a breach of privacy. An example of this actionable tort could arise in the case of test tube babies. Suppose the physician successfully fertilizes the ova in a test tube and implants the fertilized ova into the carrying mother's womb. The mother has a normal pregnancy and the baby is apparently normal at birth. If the physician divulges his accomplishment to the news media, the child and the child's family will be subjected to immediate and subsequent invasions of privacy. The child may carry the stigma of "test tube baby" throughout his life.

Mental or Emotional Distress. This tort may be alleged where the injured party experiences anxiety and other types of emotional harm as a result of a physician's acts. It is often a difficult tort to prove because it presupposes the physician's intentional infliction of emotional harm. In addition, it is necessary to prove damages and some jurisdictions do not allow recovery for mental distress alone. In these jurisdictions, mental suffering must be accompanied by physical injury.

Interference with the Marital Relationship. In an action for interference in marital relations between the spouses the defendant must directly and intentionally interfere. For example, the defendant must cause a loss of consortium (the exculsive right to the services of the spouse, and to his or her society, companionship, and conjugal affection). This tort is primarily of interest in the discussion of sterilization cases in that one spouse could sue a third party for loss of conjugal affection if such sterilization were to render one impotent or sterile. Impotence would obviously interfere with the marital relationship and it is possible that sterilization would likewise interfere with the marital relationship if the inability to procreate were to affect the relationship between the spouses.

Consent. Consent is so important in any discussion of tort law because it acts to negative the existence of any tort in the first instance. Consent is derived from a fundamental common law principle that <u>volenti non fit injuria</u> ("to one who is willing, no wrong is done"). Stated in today's language, it can be said that one who intentionally takes an action that affects the body or mind of another without the legally valid consent of that person is liable for damages unless there is some specific legal justification for taking such action. Furthermore for consent to operate as a valid defense it must be voluntary and informed.

In order to avoid civil liability, a physician or surgeon cannot under normal circumstances perform surgery or undertake medical treatment without first obtaining the patient's consent to act. In addition, this consent must be knowing, educated, and voluntary. The physician therefore has a duty to properly explain a contemplated procedure, treatment, or operation as well as the risks involved. And the explanation must be such that the patient can reasonably understand so that the consent will be knowledgeable and hence informed. Or to explain informed consent slightly differently, a physician or surgeon has a duty to inform a patient in lay terms concerning any proposed treatment so that the patient has an opportunity to ask questions and to reasonably understand the decision he will have to make. Consent is not informed if the physician or surgeon withholds information concerning the risks involved in the treatment, the nature of the treatment, or the results that may be reasonably expected. Thus, where the repercussions of a given medical procedure are extremely uncertain informed consent is particularly impossible to obtain.

Consent may be obtained in three ways. First, a patient who consents orally or in writing gives his express consent. Secondly, implied consent can be determined from the actions and conduct of a patient who knowingly accepts the recommended surgery or treatment. Thirdly, consent is sometimes implied in law where a patient cannot give his consent but medical delay would be detrimental to the patient (e.g. emergency situation).

The implied in law consent presents the question of whether there should be exceptions to the informed consent requirement in certain instances. The following are cases in point. (1) The person is unconscious. (2) The person is mentally incompetent and there is no known representative. (3) A child needs emergency treatment and the parents are unknown or cannot be reached. (4) A patient's knowledge of his illness (e.g., he has an incurable disease) might worsen his condition.

In the specific context of experimental medical prodecures and treatment, the informed consent requirement protects the individual's right to decide questions that may affect his very life. In addition, the requirement forces the researcher to review the safeguards he uses in his medical procedures and protects him from civil (and criminal) liability. And finally, the requirement increases the public awareness of human research.

The requirement of informed consent should perhaps be even more stringently applied to the experimental situation than to the general medically therapeutic situation because where the procedure is experimental and dangerous there is a greater possibility that the subject will suffer serious harm.

A final consideration concerning the informed consent requirement becomes more prominent as medical science advances. Namely, the more the medical person knows the more knowledge he will be required to impart to the patient. At some point it would seem that patient management as well as the demand on the medical professional's time might present legitimate problems for the medical person. Simultaneously, the more complex medical advancements become the more the patient will have to depend on the medical professional to make the ultimate decision concerning the patient's welfare. It is therefore suggested that the legal requirement of informed consent may become a mere ritual that recognizes the patient's humanity rather than a requirement that retains substantive meaning.

Contract Law

A contract is a legally binding agreement. But let us briefly elaborate upon that succint definition. When two or more parties enter into an agreement that in some way affects their relationships with one another, a contract has been formed. However, for the contract to be enforceable at law, certain legal formalities and requisites must have been met. Parties may generally contract to do or refrain from doing anything that is not illegal.

Both contract law and tort law are governed by civil as opposed to criminal law. However, contract law basically differs from tort law in that contractual duties are defined by the contractual parties themselves, whereas tort duties are defined by general law, regardless of the desires of the parties in a tort action. The theories of contractual liability for human experimentation (or traditional medical malpractice) are less numerous than are tort theories. Contractual liability of a doctor to his patient is usually difficult to prove because the plaintiff must prove that a contract did exist.

A doctor may of course make a contract with his patient or with the human subject of an experiment. He could contractually obligate himself to accomplish a specific result or he could guarantee that particular consequences would not arise, and so forth. If the physician put these terms into writing an express contract could be proved. Likewise, should the doctor expressly warrant particular results of his treatment orally, a contract could be found to exist. As a practical matter, however, physicians rarely make such contracts with patients.

Therefore, other theories of contract must be alleged by

the plaintiff. The plaintiff might sue on the basis that the physician/patient relationship is inherently a contractual one which need not be expressed. Or, if a particular medical treatment or experiment yields negative results of which the patient was not forewarned, the plaintiff might allege an implied warranty of success based upon contract law. Thus, we understand the importance of disclosure of risk and possible failure by the doctor. We must remember then that the following bases of contractual liability presuppose the existence of a contract, which is often extremely difficult to prove.

Breach of Contract. A breach of contract results from a breach of duty toward those parties specified by the contract. The duty is generally thought of as the obligations to be performed. Thus a breach of contract may also be defined as the failure to perform the obligations of a contract. Hence, we see that as long as the contracting parties uphold their ends of the bargain, no legal consequences arise. Legal consequences only begin to accrue if and when one of the parties breaks his side of the agreement.

To illustrate a breach of contract in a human experimentation situation, let us assume that a surgeon has told the worried parents of a mentally retarded twelve-year-old boy that he has perfected a procedure of transplanting various parts of the brain. He has repeatedly guaranteed the parents, in the presence of several mutual friends, that his operation would reverse the child's mental retardation. Since he has not been able to find other human subjects, the surgeon has even offered to perform the operation cost-free if the parents will permit him to operate on their son. Assuming that certain legal formalities could be found to exist, we might have here an express oral contract. Let us suppose that we do have one. We could have a breach of this contract if one of two subsequent events occurred.

First, let us suppose that the parents appear at the surgeon's office and tell him they are willing to have the transplant performed on their son. The surgeon develops a sudden case of "cold feet" and refuses to perform the operation. The parents could allege a breach of contract.

Or, if the surgeon proceeded with the transplant and the child survived the operation, but the child's condition of mental retardation was not reversed, an action for breach of contract might lie. Suppose, in fact, the child totally lost his main functioning powers and emerged as a "vegetable." Here, the doctor's repeated warranty that his operation could reverse the child's mental retardation was breached and the parents could sue for breach of contract in this instance.

Misrepresentation. Misrepresentation may be defined as a false statement concerning a material fact in a contract that misleads the party to whom the false statement was made. Misrepresentations may be fraudulent or innocent. A fraudulent misrepresentation is one wherein an actual honest belief in the veracity of the statement is missing; an innocent misrepresentation is one in which the actual honest belief in the truth of the statement is present.

If we think of a set of facts in which a contract to cure exists, and a medical professional makes a false statement that is an honest mistake of judgment, he has a fair chance of not being held for misrepresentation. On the other hand, if he knowingly misrepresents a fact concerning the outcome of his treatment, he may be held liable in contract for fraudulent misrepresentation. (Note this is close to the tort action for fraud and misrepresentation).

Conclusion

Dealing legally with human experimentation by way of the common law has positive and negative ramifications. On the positive side is the fact that the common law has a great deal of built-in flexibility. Therefore, the complex problems involved in human experimentation can be decided on a case by case basis after due consideration of all the facts and law. This flexibility of the common law leads to two further positive consequences. In the first place, human experimentation cases will be decided in the present rather than being predecided. This has the advantage of allowing for the expansiveness of medical research. Secondly, the common law leaves the problems of responsibility for human experimentation with the medical profession. And this is perhaps where the responsibility should remain, because medical investigators have the specialized knowledge and training to shoulder the responsibility. That is to say, medical investigators are in a better position to evaluate the potential risks involved in human experimentation. Although looking to the common law thus places the primary obligation of guarding itself within the ranks of the medical profession, it simultaneously prevents unnecessary restrictions externally imposed by persons who are less familiar with complex medical scientific problems and their consequences.

On the negative side, one might point out that the common law is evolutionary and it usually takes years for the law to become well settled in a given area. Thus the law of human experimentation will continue to be uncertain and evasive of definitive guidelines. But paradoxically, a typical consequence of the common law is that after an area of the law finally is well settled it often becomes entrenched and rigid. It is a question, then, whether the common law is effectively equipped for dealing with matters of experimentation, wherein new discoveries can occur very rapidly, if the common law principle of precedent tends toward rigidity.

Finally, members of the medical profession may not want the conflicting responsibilities of protecting the interests of society and protecting themselves when experimentation with human beings results in unforeseeable disasters. It may be demanding too much to require that medical investigators exercise a self-policing function for at least three reasons: (1) the individual researcher may be part of an investigation team and may not realize the extent of the individual participation in the overall experiment; (2) there is a margin of human error for which a person who acts in good faith should not be held liable; and (3) persons often become so involved in particular tasks that they are unable to view their relationships to the tasks in an objective manner. Medical professionals as human beings seek form, guidance, and answers. Perhaps they do not wish to be in the position of making continual unilateral decisions. They may prefer laws that would serve as prospective measuring sticks for their behavior. If the laws are clear, once they have the significant information concerning a human experiment, they can choose to proceed with the experiment or to refrain from the experiment in light of the legal risks they might be taking.

Statutory Law

Statutory law consists of the acts or session laws that the various state legislatures or the United States Congress enact. Those acts or session laws that are in force are codified into state statutes or codes. On the federal level, the acts of Congress are found in codified form known as the United States Code.

There are those legal thinkers who believe that human experimentation is one of those scientific areas that is moving too rapidly and that there are consequently ramifications that are potentially too serious to leave for the evolution of the common law. They suggest that with the cloning of a human being just around the corner, the law must be prepared in advance in order to answer the legal questions that cloning will present. To enact laws that could presuppose various situations would be one attempt at answering many of the questions in advance.

Opponents of statutory enactments as a means of averting disastrous consequences from human experimentation give rational support for their arguments. For example, state legislatures are not scientifically oriented and, thus, the adoption of statutes by the various legislatures would not ensure that the optimal scientific considerations were evaluated. There could be vast variations in the types of legislation adopted by the several states thereby causing many problems in conflicts of law. But under ordinary circumstances it would seem beneficial if scientific advancement were not confused and impeded by state lines. Yet, impediments there could be if state legislatures adopt laws independently.

Further, statutory law opponents might say that statutory law is much too inflexible to handle the legal problems involved in human experimentation. And finally, they might suggest that legislators would be wasting their own time and the taxpayers' money in attempting to guage future developments in the area of human experimentation. They might suggest that gazing into a crystal ball might be more productive than trying to foresee accurately the many possible permutations to which human experimentation might lead.

Even here, however, one might come up with a counterargument. Laws enacted by the various states as well as laws enacted by the United States Congress are subject to judicial construction or interpretation. This means that the state judiciaries and the United States federal courts look to the legislative intent in interpreting laws. It is conceded that some bad statutes have been permitted to remain on the books where the courts have left the repeal or amendment of the statute to the legislative branches. And yet, in those instances where a state or federal statute is harmful or simply "all wet," the United States Constitution provides the machinery whereby the validity of the statute may be finally decided by the United States Supreme Court. Therefore, a "bad" statute may be ultimately struck down as unconstitutional. Thus statutory law cannot be described as immovable.

Once all the arguments and counterarguments for and against statutory regulation of human experimentation are presented, we at least comprehend that the statutory method of regulation is one possibility. In addition, we realize that statutes cannot stand on their own. Once there is a legal issue concerning the validity of a given statute, its life course and even its longevity depend upon judicial interpretation. Here we see the interrelationship between case law and statutory law. And perhaps it occurs to us that regulation of human experimentation via statutory law has the advantages or disadvantages of potential consideration by two governmental branches--the legislative and the judicial.

Statutory law does not lend itself to the same kind of dissection as did common law or case law. The multiplicity of state and federal jurisdictions prohibit a state by state analysis of statutes relating to human experimentation. Thus we must take a different approach to statutory law. We shall do so by first considering generally the possible theories of criminal liability. As previously mentioned, most criminal law is now statutory in the United States. We can therefore only speak in broad generalities and we must keep in mind the fact that the state statutes of each jurisdiction have to be consulted to ascertain the exact laws in a given state.

Criminal Liability

Although no state has at yet brought criminal charges against an experimenter if he has obtained informed consent from his subject, criminal liability may be imposed on an experimenter if he totally disregards the rights of his subject. For example, the experimenter must follow stringent precautions to insure that the experiment is conducted as safely as possible, inform the subject of all possible risks, and obtain the subject's consent free of any type of coercion. Otherwise the experimenter is potentially liable on the basis of criminal law. Realistically speaking however, in light of current policy considerations evidenced by judicial decisions and legislation as well as the increased caution with which medical experimenters will have to proceed in view of the recent federal regulation of human experimentation, the possibility of a criminal prosecution resulting from voluntary experimentation is illusory.

Administrative Law

Administrative law is law that is promulgated by an administrative agency. It may be substantive law or procedural law.

Societal evolution creates new considerations. For example,

movement from an agriculture to an industry-based society created labor relations problems that were unwieldy for Congress to handle. Therefore, Congress created a special agency, the National Labor Relations Board, to deal with unfair labor practices. Once an area of law needs constant supervision and expertise in order to administer uniform justice, the Congress may create an administrative agency to deal with that area of law by way of an enabling statute. State and municipal governments generally create administrative agencies (or boards, or commissions) in a similar fashion. Therefore, we can say that administrative agencies are created by statute, by executive order authorized by statute, by state constitutional provision, or by municipal ordinance.

To simplify, let us consider the federal government's creation of administrative agencies. Congress enacts a statute that confers or delegates its powers to an administrative agency. After its creation, the agency itself makes rules, adjudicates, advises, supervises, prosecutes, and regulates in the area of the law delegated to it. It may be said, then, that Congress creates administrative agencies to develop the detailed rules and regulations necessary to execute the general regulatory policies of Congress. Once the agency's rules and regulations are adopted they have the force of law and are treated as statutes. Thus, functionally, administrative agencies have a legislative role. In addition to making rules and regulations, the agencies also administer (hence administrative agencies) them. They may also be said to have an executive function. For example, they issue licenses (e.g., to sell alcoholic beverages), distribute public benefits (e.g., veterans' benefits), mediate private disputes (e.g., settle working wage and hour controversies), investigate statutory violations, etc.

And finally, administrative agencies exercise judicial functions. They may hear legal controversies and issue enforceable decisions and orders concerning these controversies. These administrative decisions and orders are then subject to judicial review by appellate courts. Even though judicial review of administrative decisions is restricted, it is an important tool to be used after administrative proceedings have failed.

The above brief discussion of administrative law is relevant for two reasons. First of all, it is necessary to understand the hybrid nature of administrative law--its legislative, executive, and judicial functions. Otherwise the reader may not understand that not all law relating to human experimentation is statutory or judge-made. Secondly, it is necessary to emphasize the role of administrative law considering the recent enactment of Public Law 93-348 (88 Stat. 342) by the United States Congress. That law, which may be found in the Appendix, has established an administrative agency called the National Commission for the Protection of Human Subjects of Biomedical and Behavioral Research. Although the commission is so new at this point in time that it is impossible to discuss its exact duties because they have not yet been formulated, it is known that the Congressional intent is for the commission to issue policies and procedures that will protect all human subjects of biomedical or behavioral research programs, demonstrations, and activities.

Conclusion

The foregoing discussion of common law, statutory law, and administrative law should be useful to the reader as an introduction to the possibilities that exist for regulating the law of human experimentation. As pointed out above, the common law method is that which has been traditionally used for regulation of medical malpractice and thus has been superimposed upon human experimentation questions. Federal statutory law has recently been enacted and may eventually encompass the comprehensive regulation of human experimentation. (See Appendix G for the text of Public Law 93-358.) At the present time, however, legislative enactments are also reserved to the states. It should be noted, however, that state regulation of the various areas of human experimentation may be more confusing and obtrusive than helpful. Finally, administrative law may be the ultimate answer for the control of human experimentation within the United States. A federal administrative body has been established by the above referred-to legislation. It will promulgate rules and regulations concerning the complex matters involved in the issue of human experimentation. That administrative body, the National Commission for the Protection of Human Subjects of Biomedical and Behavioral Research, will have the expert personnel to deal with the specialized subject of human experimentation. The commission will eventually be composed of members of the fields of medicine, law, ethics, theology, biological science, social science, philosophy, humanities, health administration, government, and public affairs.

The current situation, in which all three types of legal regulation occur simultaneously, is likely to continue for some time. Since it is virtually impossible to remove all human experiments from at least some type of state control, state statutes will undoubtedly continue to issue and these statutes will be construed by state courts. It is less likely that each state will establish administrative agencies to handle human experimentation matters because the volume of state litigation and involvement is unlikely to warrant the state expense of such specialized agencies.

In essence then, the following pattern is likely to control the law of human experimentation in the foreseeable future. States will promulgate laws that the state courts will interpret. If a federal constitutional issue arises out of a state action, the United States Supreme Court will become the final arbiter of such statutes. On the federal level, national legislation has been promulgated in an initial attempt to control human experimentation. The national administrative agency established by that legislation will regulate an increasing number of human experimentation issues. The commission will control matters that affect several states. That is, it will control any kind of experiment that receives federal monies and it can be expected to exercise control over any materials (such as "spare parts" of human beings) or any personnel traveling in the stream of interstate commerce by virtue of the commerce clause of the United States Constitution.

In the chapters that follow, specific areas of human experimentation will be discussed. Perhaps the reader should consider what he believes would be the optimal method of legal control--judge-made law, statutory law, or administrative law as well as state versus federal law--in view of the unique questions inherent in each subject area.

Chapter 4

STERILIZATION

The news media warn that a world-wide food shortage is imminent. Even though some countries have reached or are rapidly approaching zero population growth, experts tell us that this must become a global phenomenon. We read that time is of the essence--that this enormous decrease in the birth rate must happen immediately. Some authorities even suggest that it is too late to reverse the geometric population explosion because the earth will shortly be unable to provide resources for the people who presently exist. Few of us have the mathematical and scientific skills to individually reach a conclusion concerning the soundness of these gloomy predictions and still fewer of us have clairvoyant skills that might enable us to reach a conclusion by a different means.

For the majority of Americans, with incredibly high standards of living compared with the majority in many countries, the Malthusian theory of economics was a principle passed over lightly in high schools or college. And then came the winter of 1974. Automobiles waiting their turns at the gasoline pump were lined up for city blocks in some places in the United States. There was talk of heating-fuel shortages. Some people began buying commercial fuel storage tanks for their back yards. The scare was on. Whether or not the fuel shortage was real or a hoax, people were awakened to the possibility that natural resources are not undiminishable commodities. Even those persons with the unflagging belief that technology will *always* be around to rescue the human race were unable to produce a synthetic fuel source behind any bush.

One of the consequences of these warnings of shortages is a pervasive feeling that the earth cannot support its inhabitants. This feeling must surely make more people think seriously about family planning and population control. And, in any serious consideration of population control, the possibility of sterilization must be considered.

Sterility in human beings is the inability to reproduce the species. Persons of either sex may be naturally sterile. Sterilization, however, implies the artificial inducement of sterility.

Sterilization may be accomplished surgically in either the male or female.

In the female, the surgical procedure for achieving sterilization is one of the following: (1) severing and tying the cut ends of the Fallopian tubes (tubal ligation or salpingectomy); (2) removal of the ovaries; or (3) removal of the uterus (hysterectomy). The surgical procedures for sterilizing the male are: (1) severing and tying the cut ends of the tubes that carry sperm from the testicles to the uretha (vasectomy); or (2) removal of the testicles (castration).

The vasectomy in the male is the simplest operation surgically since it only requires local anesthetic and can be performed in an outpatient clinic or physician's office. In addition, there are fewer postoperative problems than in the other four surgical procedures listed above. The problem with performing vasectomies arises because physicians do not know whether or not they are legal. Sterilization in females are performed for a variety of reasons, and if the sterilization is simply for the purpose of being unable to reproduce, this reason need not be documented. In the male, however, sterilization cannot be hidden because a vasectomy has but one purpose.

The increased interest in sterilization has led to a relatively new and simple technique for sterilizing women. The technique is called laparoscopy and it is increasingly replacing the conventional tubal ligation where the abdomen is cut open and the Fallopian tubes tied. In the laparoscopy a woman's tubes are located with a visualizing instrument and are then cauterized with a forceps inserted through small abdominal incisions. The laparoscopy has the advantages of being less expensive and less traumatic than are the major surgery and long convalescence of a conventional tubal ligation.

It is difficult to consider the legal as well as the ethical problems inherent in sterilization operations unless one separates compulsory (generally involuntary) from voluntary sterilization.

Compulsory Sterilization

Compulsory sterilization may also be referred to as mandatory sterilization. In the case of compulsory sterilization, there are statutes that compel the state to sterilize persons if certain conditions are present. Although compulsory and involuntary sterilization are not synonymous, they usually coincide. That is, theoretically a person could volunteer to be sterilized before or concurrent with the issuance of a state decree requiring sterilization of the individual. To illustrate, assume an epileptic did not wish to transmit his hereditary disease (in spite of medical advances that enable epileptics to live normal lives if they are under proper medication). If the epileptic sought sterilization voluntarily in a state that compels the sterilization of epileptics, this would be an instance of a voluntary compulsory sterilization. However, most compulsory sterilization cases are not so cut and dried--from the point of view of individual rights.

The sterilization of an epileptic, whether voluntary or involuntary is an example of a eugenic sterilization. A eugenic sterilization may be defined as one designed to prevent the conception of children who might be mentally or physically defective due to hereditary factors. Other reasons for eugenic sterilization are the prevention of the conception of children likely to have criminal or sexually deviant tendencies.

In addition to eugenic reasons, some states are legally permitted to perform compulsory sterilization to improve any physical or mental condition in the person to be sterilized, if conception would normally worsen that condition, or to insure certain societal values deemed to be in the best interest of the general public.

As of 1968 there were twenty-seven states with eugenic sterilization laws in force. This was a decrease from thirty-two states in 1942. In 1968 the feeble-minded or mentally deficient were subject to sterilization in all twenty-seven states, the mentally ill in twenty-five states, habitual criminals in seven, and "moral degenerates and sexual perverts" in seven. By 1974, the number of states with eugenic sterilization laws had decreased to 19. (See Appendices A and B.)

The impetus for most of the state statutes authorizing compulsory eugenic sterilization was a United States case, <u>Buck v. Bell</u> (274 U.S. 200), which was decided in 1927. The case arose in Virginia under the following set of facts.

Under a Virginia sterilization statute, Dr. Bell, superintendent of the State Colony for Epileptics and Feeble-Minded, was ordered to sterilize Carrie Buck, an inmate of the institution. At age seventeen, Carrie Buck was committed to the State Colony for Epileptics and Feeble-Minded. She was alleged to have the mind of a nine-year-old child. She was the mother of an illegitimate child of defective mentality. And Carrie Buck's own mother was likewise a feeble-minded person.

The state's contentions in this case were (1) that by the

laws of heredity she was the probable potential parent of socially inadequate offspring; and (2) that she would therefore have to be kept in the colony until she was naturally sterile and would thus be a charge upon the state for some thirty years. On the other hand, she would be given her freedom to leave the colony if she were sterilized surgically.

Thus, the state reasoned, the compulsory sterilization would serve both the state (relieving it of its custodial burden for Carrie Buck and any other feeble-minded children she might bear) and Carrie Buck (allowing her to "go free").

However, Carrie Buck's guardian contested the constitutionality of the Virginia act on the grounds that it did not provide due process of law as guaranteed by the Fourteenth Amendment to the Constitution of the United States.

The United States Supreme Court upheld the validity of the Virginia statute and in an often quoted passage, Justice Holmes set the standard of state control of the individual's right to procreate as he wishes. Speaking for the majority, he said:

> We have seen more than once that the public welfare may call upon the best citizens for their lives. It would be strange if it could not call upon those who already sap the strength of the State for these lesser sacrifices, often not felt to be such by those concerned, in order to prevent our being swamped with incompetence. It is better for all the world, if instead of waiting to execute degenerate offspring for crime, or to let them starve for their imbecility, society can prevent those who are manifestly unfit from continuing their kind. The principle that sustains compulsory vaccination is broad enough to cover cutting the Fallopian tubes. Jacobson v. Massachusetts, (197 U.S. 11). Three generations of imbeciles are enough.

Jacobson v. Massachusetts was decided in 1905. It held that the enacting of a compulsory vaccination law is within the police power of the state.

An Oregon court upheld the validity of its sterilization statute in a recent decision in Cook v. State (Or. App., 495 P. 2d 768) decided in 1972. The plaintiff was a seventeen-year-old girl who had a history of severe emotional disturbance. While in a state hospital she engaged in indiscriminate sexual behavior. A petition was thus filed with the Board of Social Protection that ordered sterilization of the girl. This order was based on a psychiatrist's uncontradicted testimony that the plaintiff would never be able to provide a child with necessary parental guidance and that she would be likely to abuse her child due to her mental illness and retardation.

The plaintiff contended that the Oregon statute denied her equal protection under the Fourteenth Amendment. The basis of her argument was that the statute in effect discriminates only against those mentally ill persons who are poor, since it is only their children who will become neglected or dependent. The court rejected plaintiff's argument, however, holding the statute non-discriminatory between rich and poor on its face. The court deemed the purpose of the statute to be the protection of the state from public charges. It reasoned further that if there is overwhelming evidence that a potential parent will not be able to furnish a proper environment for a child due to his own mental illness or retardation, the state may order sterilization.

Over the years a considerable number of cases have tested the validity of state sterilization statutes. The cases have contested the various state statutes under the following grounds: (1) whether the statutes are valid as being within the police power of the state; (2) whether the statutes inflict cruel or unusual punishment; (3) whether the statutes are in compliance with state or federal guarantees of due process of law; (4) whether the statutes are constitutionally vague; (5) whether the statutes are in compliance with state or federal guarantees of equal protection of the law or prohibitions of arbitrary class legislation; and (6) whether the statutes constituted an unlawful delegation of legislative, judicial or quasi-judicial power to an administrative body.

Although a few cases have held the statutes invalid under certain circumstances, the majority of the cases have found the state statutes to be valid. The cases in the area of compulsory sterilization clearly support the conclusion that the courts will allow involuntary sterilization for eugenic reasons unless such sterilizations can be shown to be invidious class discrimination. The apparent rationale behind the court's support of involuntary sterilization statutes is that there is a compelling state interest in protecting the public from having to support eugenically defective persons and that the state may therefore enact and enforce compulsory controls to preserve that interest.

Today, we see that compulsory sterilization has been performed only for eugenic reasons. But the "compelling state interest" rationale forces us to look at another possibility. In any form of control, the law must use involuntary controls where voluntary controls are not effective. And, once the law has recognized a "compelling state interest" in matters of procreation, we should consider what that means in terms of population control.

Adherents of involuntary programs for population control have proposed that the state step in after a couple has had two children. The proposals suggest punitive measures such as stiff fines and/or imprisonment for having more than two children. Most proponents of involuntary birth control admit to the undesirability of stringent punitive steps to impede population growth. Yet, they maintain that it is the only expedient way of dealing with the world's grave population crisis. They therefore suggest statutory implementation of involuntary control of population.

After state fines and imprisonment, it requires only a cushioned step further to suggest that as soon as a second child is born to a couple, both parents are required to be immediately sterilized. Although no legislation has been proposed along these lines, the cases following the Buck v. Bell reasoning could be used as precedents for legal arguments supporting involuntary sterilization statutes for population control purposes.

Voluntary Sterilization

Voluntary sexual sterilizations are those requested by the individual to undergo the operation or those to which the individual consents. Consent is the essential legal element separating voluntary from involuntary sterilization.

Generally, voluntary sterilizations are performed for either of two reasons. First of all, the reason may be the therapeutic or medical interest of the patient. That is, where pregnancy would endanger the life, or physical or mental health, of the patient therapeutic sterilization may be performed. In this first instance of therapeutic sterilization the patient is always female. However, there are therapeutic situations in which the future avoidance of pregnancy is not the primary reason for the sterilization. For example, vasectomies are sometimes performed on the male in the treatment of prostatic cancer. Or, diseased ovaries or uterus are removed from female patients. Secondly, the reason for performing a voluntary sterilization may be solely as a means of contraceptive convenience. In this case, either the male or the female may surgically undergo a voluntary sterilization for contraceptive purposes.

A voluntary contraceptive sterilization is usually initiated by the individual in the United States. In some countries that are extremely overcrowded (India for example), voluntary contraceptive sterilizations are promoted by the government through tax, welfare, and insurance incentives, or lump sums of money are offered as inducements for sterilization. Therefore there may be a question of the voluntariness of the sterilization where systematic rewards are offered. But we can most likely at least find consent as it is legally defined. Therefore these government-encouraged sterilizations fall in the same category of voluntary sterilizations as do therapeutic sterilizations for medical reasons, in that both presume the consent of the individual to be sterilized.

Legality of Voluntary Sterilization. First of all, as a purely practical matter, it must be noted that voluntary sterilization is not always available to all persons requesting that the procedure be performed. For example, one spouse is required to consent to the sterilization of the other. Considering society's current interest in promoting the stability of the marital relationship, the interspousal consent would seem reasonable. A less reasonable de facto restriction placed upon voluntary sterilizations is that which is often forced upon single persons. Many physicians are reluctant to perform sterilizations for merely contraceptive means upon young, single persons of either sex. But it is more difficult for a young, single woman to obtain a voluntary contraceptive sterilization than it is for a young, single man to do so. Physicians urge the woman to wait because she may want to bear children at some future date. Some physicians simply refuse to perform such sterilizations either taking an in loco parentis stance or fearing legal reprisals should the person change her mind in the future. Furthermore, even where a young, single person can find a physician who is willing to perform the contraceptive sterilization, he must also overcome the obstacle of certain clinic and hospital regulations that further obstruct one's efforts to consent to such a sterilization. As pointed out above, there may be a legitimate fear on the part of the doctor that the single person may decide to bear children in the future and either take legal action himself or if later married, encourage the spouse to bring the action against the doctor. However, it is almost 100 percent certain that such a claim would be summarily dismissed as long as consent had been obtained from the voluntarily sterilized person. It seems, rather, that the reluctance of physicians to perform the sterilizations stems simply from a moral/value judgment that single persons (particularly women) do not have the right not to bear children.

At the present time no state has enacted a statute that prohibits voluntary sterilization. However, at least two states limit voluntary sterilization. According to Colorado law, a physician must consent to a voluntary sterilization before it can be performed. In Utah, there is a state statute that limits voluntary sterilizations to cases involving medical necessity. The statute is currently being judicially tested. But until the statute is revoked, physicians will perform voluntary contraceptive sterilizations at their own peril.

Presumably no state would pass legislation restricting voluntary sterilization for sound medical reasons. And presumably no state could pass legislation restricting voluntary contraceptive sterilization that would not be overturned by the United States Supreme Court. This position is based upon two United States Supreme Court decisions that would undoubtedly serve as precedents in any contest concerning the individual's rights to voluntary contraceptive sterilization. These decisions are Griswold v. Connecticut, (381 U.S. 479 (1965)) and Roe v. Wade, (410 U.S. 113 (1973)).

In Griswold v. Connecticut, there was a Connecticut statute making the use of contraceptives a criminal offense. Appellant Griswold was the executive director of the Planned Parenthood League of Connecticut. Appellant Buxton was a licensed physician and a professor at Yale Medical School. Buxton also acted as medical director for the Planned Parenthood League at its New Haven Center. Griswold and Buxton were arrested and convicted of being in violation of the statute by giving information, instruction, and medical advice to married persons as to the means of preventing conception. The Supreme Court of the United States reversed the ruling of the Connecticut courts. The Supreme Court held that the Connecticut statute was invalid as an unconstitutional invasion of the right of privacy of married persons. Therefore the Griswold decision upheld the individual's right to practice birth control as a constitutional right--at least in the case of married persons.

Roe v. Wade extended the individual right of privacy in contraceptive matters by sanctioning the termination of pregnancy by abortion and the right was extended to unmarried as well as married women. The plaintiff, Roe, was an unmarried pregnant woman who instituted a class action in a United States district court challenging the constitutionality of the Texas criminal abortion laws that prohibited abortion except on medical advice for the purpose of saving the mother's life. Although the court held that the Texas criminal abortion statutes were void on their face, the decision reached the United States Supreme Court because the district court would not grant an injunction against continued enforcement of the abortion statute. The Supreme Court held inter alia that state criminal abortion laws, that permit abortion only to save the mother's life, without regard to the mother's stage of pregnancy and other interests, violate the due process clause of the Fourteenth Amendment, which protects the right to privacy and includes a woman's qualified right to terminate her pregnancy. The Supreme Court qualified the woman's right to terminate her pregnancy based upon the mother's health and the viability of the fetus. The Court said that prior to the end of the first trimester of pregnancy, the state may not interfere with or regulate an attending physician's decision reached in consultation with his patient, that the patient's pregnancy be terminated. During the period ending with the first trimester and until the fetus becomes viable, the Court said the state may, if it chooses, regulate the abortion procedure in ways reasonably related to the protection of maternal health. Finally, the Court held that as soon as the fetus becomes viable, the state may prohibit abortions unless it is necessary to protect the life or health of the mother.

It would seem therefore that any state restriction upon contraception by means of voluntary sterilization would be held invalid as an invasion of privacy. Although the issue has not been decided by the United States Supreme Court, the California courts have decided the question in Jessin v. County of Shasta, (274 Cal. App. 2d 737, 79 Cal. Rptr. 359 (1969)).

The Jessins, an indigent married couple, brought an action against Shasta County, California alleging that the county was required by law to provide them with surgical sterilization. The county had refused to grant their request. The plaintiffs contended that they were parents of as many children as they could adequately support. Furthermore, the plaintiffs' complaint alleged that Shasta County's refusal to provide the sterilization constituted an arbitrary and unconstitutional discrimination against the plaintiffs because of their indigent financial status. They pointed out that voluntary sterilizations are readily available to other citizens of Shasta County who have the money to engage private physicians to perform sexual sterilization.

In its defense, the defendant, Shata County, answered that nontherapeutic surgical sterilizations are unlawful. The California Court of Appeals refused to extend the scope of medical care under publicly sponsored welfare programs to include voluntary sterilizations. But the court did adress itself to the legality of nontherapeutic surgical sterilization.

The Jessin case was decided after Griswold but before Roe. The court discussed the applicability of Griswold stating that ". . . the holding of the court [in Griswold] that the statute was invalid as an unconstitutional invasion of the right of privacy of married persons seems to declare the individual's right to practice voluntary birth control." The California court continued:

> However, we do not now need to decide the applicability of Griswold to the instant case, for we conclude that there is no legislative policy or any other overriding public policy proscribing consensual vasectomy in this state. Nor does there appear to be any other good legal reason why such a voluntary operation given competent consent, should not be performed. In fact, the few cases in this area indicate that it is an acceptable method of family planning, while Griswold indicates that it may fall within constitutional protection. . . . There being no other real controversy between the parties . . . "IT IS ADJUDGED that voluntary nontherapeutic surgical sterilization operations are legal in the state of California."

Thus, considering the Jessin California precedent, expressly holding voluntary nontherapeutic surgical sterilizations legal, as well as Roe, in which the United States Supreme Court impliedly guaranteed abortions as a means of contraception until the pregnancy reached the point wherein the health of the mother or the life of the fetus warranted consideration, it is extremely unlikely that states could legislate anti-nontherapeutic voluntary sterilization statutes that would survive a Supreme Court test.

That a hospital's barring of consensual sterilization has not survived a federal circuit court test has been proved by the case of Hathaway v. Worcester City Hospital, (475 F. 2d 701 (1st Cir. 1973). In this case the mother had had twelve pregnancies and given birth to eight live offspring. Future pregnancies were determined to be a great risk to her life. Her physician therefore recommended a therapeutic sterilization. In 1970, the appellant's hospital board of trustees barred the use of hospital facilities for the purpose of consensual sterilizations. The federal court held the hospital's prohibition on sterilizations to be violative of the equal protection clause of the Fourteenth Amendment since the hospital did not outright prohibit other surgical procedures. Citing Roe v. Wade, the court said:

> The state interests, recognized by Roe as legitimate, are far less compelling in this context. Whatever interest the state might assert in preserving the possibility of future fetuses cannot rival its interest in preserving an actual fetus, which was found sufficiently compelling to outweigh the woman's interest only at the point of viability.

Although the Hathaway decision did not decide the validity of state statutes proscribing voluntary sterilization, it did strike down the hospital's policy of not permitting consensual sterilizations. And it did so on the basis of Roe v. Wade and its companion case, Doe v. Bolton, (410 U.S. 179 (1973)), thereby adding further support and momentum to the proposition that any legislative restrictions upon voluntary sterilization--therapeutic or contraceptive--would be struck down by the United States Supreme Court.

Criminal Liability

In the states that have compulsory sterilization statutes, a physician performing surgical sterilizations will not be criminally liable whether or not he has obtained the personal consent of the patient. The foregoing statement is of course predicated on the assumption that the sterilization has been performed according to law and that the requisite state authorization for the sterilization has been obtained.

In the absence of statutes prohibiting nontherapeutic voluntary sterilization (the majority of the states), it is unlikely that a physician would be saddled with criminal liability if he used approved medical procedures, performed the sterilization nonnegligently, and had obtained the patient's informed consent. And in view of the Griswold, Roe, Jessin and Hathaway decisions discussed above, it is even unlikely that those few states with statutes permitting voluntary sterilization for medical reasons only could impose criminal liability on a physician for performing a nonnegligent consensual sterilization operation. And those states that have statutorily declared voluntary sterilizations performed without medical necessity lawful (e.g., Connecticut, Georgia, North Carolina, Oregon, Tennessee, Virginia), physicians are immune from criminal liability.

Perhaps the only kind of sterilization for which a criminal action would lie, would be one performed merely for scientific research purposes, similar to those performed at Auschwitz and Ravensbruecke concentration camps from 1941 to 1945. The sole purpose of those experiments was to find a method of mass sterilization that would cost a minimum of time and effort. Should a medical researcher resume such experiments on a small scale or a large scale (as in Nazi Germany, where thousands of persons were sterilized), such researcher would undoubtedly be liable at criminal law. The basis for criminal liability for sterilization would be mayhem or assault or both.

Mayhem. At English common law, mayhem was a crime in which a man was injured without cause and was thereby rendered less able to fight for the king or less able to defend himself. Thus a sterilization procedure (with the possible exception of castration) would not have constituted mayhem at English common law. However, modern statutory definitions of mayhem in the various jurisdictions have extended the offense of mayhem to include the disabling of any bodily member or organ or merely disfigurement. And although the English common law only applied to men, modern statutes clearly apply mayhem to women and men equally.

Assault. A criminal assault takes place when there is an overt act or an attempt to inflict immediate physical injury on another by force and violence. Although statutes vary concerning the exact elements of the offense of criminal assault they basically conform with the above definition.

Civil Liability

Whether or not a physician is criminally liable for performing sterilization operations, he is civilly liable for any harm he causes the person undergoing the sterilization. And civil liability is applicable in compulsory as well as voluntary sterilization. The physician is civilly liable for the same reasons he is generally liable in performing other surgical procedures.

Civil suits can theoretically be brought against physicians on a number of grounds, namely, civil assault, negligence, breach of contract or warranty, fraud, deceit, misrepresentation, and interference with the marital relationship. For a discussion of the above mentioned grounds, see Chapter 3, "Legal Considerations."

Conclusion

Sterilization is clearly classifiable as a subcategory of human experimentation for a variety of reasons. Although the surgical procedures themselves are hardly novel or medically unsound, the overall effect of voluntary and involuntary sterilization upon the gene pool may be considered experimental. Until recent medical advances that rendered sterilization relatively uncomplicated and safe, human beings reproduced randomly. The genetic heritage of homo sapiens resulted in offspring with varying physical and intellectual abilities. Today, the potential for sterilization can change the genetic heritage. Hypothetically, if those persons with outstanding intellectual and physical abilities choose to be sterilized, the common gene pool may be negatively affected. On the other hand, if persons with certain hereditary diseases are forced to be sterilized, this could conceivably cause other diseases and defects to appear within the common gene pool. Although the resultant selective breeding may not be actually, but rather only morally detrimental to mankind, there are experimental risks to human beings since we cannot accurately predict the outcome of such selective breeding.

A second approach to the experimental nature of sterilization occurs only in the event of sterilizations performed merely to gain scientific knowledge. Although it is possible to imagine that some few persons would submit to sterilization for science's sake alone, it is much more realistic to assume that sterilization for the sole purpose of adding to scientific knowledge would be compulsory sterilizations. As pointed out above, such sterilizations have been performed in the past--undoubtedly in instances other than in Nazi Germany. We can only hope that the cumulative decency of mankind will one day abolish even the remotest chance that such operations for solely experimental reasons are possible.

Chapter 5

FETAL EXPERIMENTATION

Fetal experimentation has recently become a subject of great medical, moral, and legal concern. Although medical researchers have been experimenting with fetuses for several years, the legal, moral, and medical controversy is relatively recent for two reasons. First, Roe v. Wade, (410 U.S. 113 (1973)), the United States Supreme Court decision that legalized abortion, has resulted in an increased number of legally aborted fetuses that are available for experimentation. Secondly, science has advanced to a point where it is possible to prolong fetal life by artificial means. Consequently several states have adopted legislation in an attempt to regulate fetal research. (See Appendix B.) And on the federal level Congress enacted a moratorium on experimentation with living fetuses (Public Law 93-348, Title II, sec. 213 (1974), known as National Research Service Award Act of 1974). (See Appendix G.)

The moral outrage manifested by antiabortion forces stems from the belief that the fetus has a spiritual existence before live birth and that it therefore has a right to life. The same belief carries over into the area of fetal experimentation. It is still impossible to scientifically prove when life begins. Since the controversy then is based upon philosophical and moral beliefs, it will continue as long as man differs in those beliefs. The heated debate stimulates one to trace through the centuries the variance of opinion as to when life begins.

Philosophical History

The philosophical question is whether life begins at conception, at live birth, or at some point between conception and live birth. The Stoics believed that life did not begin until live birth. The vast majority of adherents to Judaism accept that view, as do a large number of Protestants. Roman Catholics officially espoused the Aristotelian theory of "mediate animation"--that the fetus becomes a person at some point between conception and live birth--which was the predominant European theory of when life begins throughout the Middle Ages and the Renaissance. Aristotle's theory was the official doctrine of the Catholic church until the nineteenth century, when proponents of the "ensoulment" theory instituted the belief that life exists from the moment of conception as official Roman Catholic dogma. The "ensoulment" theory is still the official position of the Roman Catholic church. It is a view that is also held by many non-Catholics.

Legal History

The law has been reluctant to accord the fetus legal rights. The predominant legal position today is that a person's legal rights are contingent upon his live birth. The fetus then is legally recognized as a potential life whose rights vest upon live birth.

However, the history of legal recognition of the fetus in the matter of criminal abortion has taken a slightly different course. According to the English common law, an abortion became a criminal offense once the fetus "quickened." "Quickening" occurred when the movement of the fetus in utero was first perceived. This usually occurred from the sixteenth to the eighteenth week of pregnancy. There was no common law crime for prequickening abortions.

In 1803 England enacted its first criminal abortion statute. The abortion of a quick fetus was a capital offense whereas the abortion of a prequickened fetus carried lesser penalties. The quickening distinction later disappeared. In 1929 the Infant Life (Preservation) Act, 19 & 20 Geo. 5 c. 34 was promulgated. This act made the abortion of a child capable of being born alive a felony unless such abortion was performed for the purpose of preserving the life of the mother. In 1967 Parliament enacted a new abortion law, the Abortion Act of 1967, 15 & 16 Eliz. 2 c. 87. This act served to greatly liberalize the English antiabortion law.

In the United States, the English common law was in effect in almost all the states until the middle of the nineteenth century. In 1828 New York enacted an abortion law that became the model for other early antiabortion legislation. The New York law made the destruction of an unquickened fetus a misdemeanor and the destruction of a quickened fetus, second degree manslaughter. It also provided for therapeutic abortions by excusing any abortion performed for the purpose of preserving the life of the mother. In general it was not until after the Civil War that the various states began enacting legislation which was to replace the common law. Such early legislation generally kept the quickening distinction. Between the middle and late nineteenth century, the quickening distinction disappeared from most of the state statutes and the penalties for abortion increased. By the 1950s most states had banned abortion unless performed to save the life of the mother.

Medical and scientific professionals have tended to be disinterested in the "quickening" event. They have focused upon whether or not the fetus is "viable." That is, they consider the fetus a life when it is potentially capable of living outside the mother's womb with or without artificial aid. The Supreme Court adopted this scientifically oriented theory of viability of the fetus in Roe v. Wade. The Court described viability as occurring at twenty-four to twenty-eight weeks of pregnancy.

In short, until the United States Supreme Court rendered its abortion decision in Roe v. Wade, a woman had few rights in determining whether to continue her pregnancy. She had substantially greater rights at common law and throughout the major part of the nineteenth century when abortion was viewed with much less disfavor. Since abortion fell into disfavor in order to protect the prenatal rights of the fetus, the legal argument seemed somewhat specious in that the law had been so reluctant to accord the fetus any legal rights until it was born alive.

However, legal arguments notwithstanding, those persons who truly believe that life begins at conception are confronted with a moral dilemma of great magnitude. They believe that abortion is equivalent to murder of another human being. And all the legal opinion in the world will not assuage their consciences or ameliorate their feelings.

Research Perspectives

Medical experiments have been conducted upon three types of fetuses: (1) the dead fetus; (2) the fetus in utero; and (3) the live, nonviable, aborted fetus. Since few abortions are performed upon viable fetuses in the United States, fetal experimentation does not generally extend to viable fetuses.

The dead fetus. Experimentation is conducted with dead fetuses in order to detect diseases in the mother and to reduce the hazards of induced abortion. In addition, researchers are trying to determine whether or not aborted fetuses can be used as donor tissue. And dead fetuses are also used to investigate fetal abnormalities in order to prevent birth defects and disease in other fetuses.

The fetus in utero. Experiments with the fetus in utero may

or may not involve direct treatment of the fetus. For example, the mother may be treated or given drugs while the fetus is in utero and the effects of the treatment or drugs are later observed in the aborted fetus. Such procedures do not directly involve the fetus. On the other hand a procedure such as amniocentesis (a hollow needle is inserted in the abdominal wall and into the amniotic sac containing the fetus and a sample of the amniotic fluid is withdrawn) does directly involve the fetus. This procedure is used to diagnose fetal conditions such as sex-linked diseases and genetic disorders during pregnancy. The danger lies in the needle puncture of the fetus which could substantially injure a sensitive organ such as an eye.

The live, nonviable, aborted fetus. Experimentation with live, nonviable, aborted fetuses is conducted in order to study the period during which a fetus can be kept alive after abortion and/or to obtain cells or organs for laboratory or clinical use. The purposes of the above kinds of research include: (1) the development of a procedure for keeping a nonviable fetus alive outside the womb until it could reach a stage of maturity enabling it to live in a nursery; (2) the development of treatment of conditions and illnesses found in newborn infants; (3) the accumulation of information involving birth defects, the rate of neonatal mortality, and other physiological data; (4) the transplantation of fetal tissue; (5) the collection of biochemical data; and (6) the development and production of vaccines.

The Legal Response

A speedy legal response has been made in relation to fetal experimentation. There has been legislation concerning the subject on the federal and state levels. In addition, the Department of Health, Education, and Welfare has issued guidelines concerning the matter.

Federal legislative response. As mentioned above, the ninety-third Congress enacted Public Law 93-348 (National Research Service Award Act of 1974). The law has halted research on "a living human fetus, before or after the induced abortion of such fetus, unless such research is done for the purpose of assuring the survival of such fetus." This moratorium on fetal research will be in effect until the National Commission for the Protection of Human Subjects of Biomedical and Behavioral Research has made its recommendations in the area of fetal experimentation.

In addition legislation has been introduced in Congress that would amend the United States Constitution in order to prohibit fetal abortion. For example, on May 31, 1973, Senator James L. Buckley of New York proposed Senate Joint Resolution 119. The proposed amendment follows:

> With respect to the right to life, the word 'person', as used in this article and in the fifth and fourteenth articles of amendment to the Constitution of the United States, applies to all human beings, including their unborn offspring at every stage of their biological development, irrespective of age, health, function, or condition of dependency.
>
> This article shall not apply in an emergency when a reasonable medical certainty exists that continuation of the pregnancy will cause the death of the mother.
>
> Congress and the several States shall have power to enforce this article by appropriate legislation within their respective jurisdictions.

Federal administrative response. On August 23, 1974, the Department of Health, Education and Welfare published proposed regulations on fetal research that is supported by federal funds. The proposed regulations would disallow all research activity on a fetus or pregnant woman unless the activity would benefit the particular fetus or respond to the health needs of the particular mother. The rules would, however, allow research activity conducted as part of a procedure to terminate pregnancy if the purpose of the research were to evaluate or improve methods of prenatal diagnosis, methods of prevention of premature birth, or methods of intervention to offset the effects of genetic abnormality or congenital injury.

Further, the regulations require that (1) the researcher may not participate in the abortion, (2) a nonviable fetus that is expelled whole can be used for research only after appropriate animal research has been completed, (3) the mother must give her consent, (4) the father must give his consent if his whereabouts are known, and (5) any research must be conducted in compliance with all local laws.

State legislative response. At least ten states have enacted statutes that restrict or prohibit human fetal experimentation. The statutes vary considerably. Since fetal experimentation has proved medically productive, it seems that the state legislatures may be overreacting. The overbroad, often vague legislation would indicate that scientific and expert medical opinions may not have been sought by the state legislators. At this point medical researchers can only hope that the other state legislatures will not continue to act with such haste. It would seem reasonable for states to merely call a moratorium on fetal research and to wait for the National Commission for the Protection of Human Subjects of Biomedical and Behavioral Research to make its recommendations. The commission should have the expertise and the funds available to it to do a medically sounder investigation than can any of the state legislatures.

Appendix C cites the statutes of the ten states that have enacted fetal experimentation legislation. Appendix D is the text of the Massachusetts law that restricts human fetal experimentation. That recent state statute has received a good deal of publicity in scientific literature and it is an example of rather comprehensive and explicit legislation in the area of fetal experimentation.

Chapter 6

TRANSPLANTATION

Transplantation involving human beings takes place when tissues are removed from one's own body and placed elsewhere on that same body, or when tissues are removed from the body of another person or an animal and placed in or on the body of a human recipient. The transplanted tissues are generally any of the following: heart, kidney, cornea, liver, pancreas, lung, intestine, artery, skin, or bone marrow.

Transplants are medically categorized as follows. (1) <u>Autografts</u>. An autograft involves a tissue transplant where the tissue donor is also the tissue recipient. A skin graft is an example of the autograft. (2) <u>Homograft</u>. A homograft is performed where tissue is removed from one donor and transplanted in a genetically unrelated recipient. The donor and recipient must be members of the same species (two humans, for example). (3) <u>Isograft</u>. An isograft involves the removal of tissue from a donor and transplanting it in the donor's identical twin. Since the donor and recipient are obviously members of the same species in this instance, an isograft may be seen as a special category of the homograft. (4) <u>Heterograft</u>. A heterograft is performed in cases where the tissue donor is of one species and the recipient of another. An example of a heterograft is a tissue transplant between an animal and a human.

Transplantation as Experimentation

Skin grafts require transplantation of tissue. However, they are generally therapeutic and the risks are generally known so they cannot be said to be experimental. Likewise, organ transplants are more and more common and certainly medically approved for therapeutic purposes. However, many medical specialists still consider the transplantation of vital organs of an experimental nature. This is particularly true of the heart transplant.

It has been but eight years since the first human heart transplant was performed on December 3, 1967. In Capetown, South Africa, Dr. Christian Barnard and his surgical assistants gave Louis Washkansky a new heart. This event led to a great deal of legal literature concerning what the legal consequences of transplantation might be. Since that first cardiac transplant medical science in the area of organ transplants has advanced rapidly. As a matter of fact, the area is constantly being refined and perfected. And yet, the area is still considered experimental in a therapeutic sense because there are still medical problems of tissue rejection, of transplanting organs of sizes different from the original organ (this is particularly problematic in the case of heart transplants), etc. Additionally, tissue transplantation has a great potential for nontherapeutic experimentation. Can a person be held together by organs and body parts from a spare-parts bank? In other words, is a Frankenstein creation a possibility? Other hypothetical questions could be framed. However, most surgical transplant teams seem to be highly skilled and to have noble intentions in performing transplants. However, remembering the maxim that "the physician experiments at his peril," we shall look at the legal problems inherent in therapeutic transplants, in order to lay a legal foundation for problems that could arise in case of nontherapeutic, totally experimental transplants.

Legal Questions

Broadly speaking there are three categories of persons with primary interests requiring protection in the transplant situation --the transplant donor, the transplant recipient, and the physician. The secondary protectible interests include those of the spouses and next of kin of both the transplant donor and recipient; and the rights and liabilities of the non-decision-making medical professionals involved in a transplant, as well as those of the hospital where the transplant was performed.

The specific legal issues involved in transplantation are many. We can ask any of the following questions: (1) Who may donate organs or entire bodies? (I.e., may a minor or incompetent donate his tissue in the same way as an adult? (2) How does one express his intention to donate his organs or his entire body? (3) In the case of a cadaver donor, how should the law define death? (4) Where a situation arises in which there are more needy tissue and organ recipients than there are donors, which recipients have priority rights to the donated tissues and organs? (5) How does an organ donor consent to removal of his tissues before death? After death? (6) In the event of the cadaver donor, what are the rights of his spouse and next of kin? (7) Does the cadaver donor have inalienable rights that would preclude the use of his tissues in the absence of his own consent? (8) How will spare-parts banks be regulated? Many of the questions will be answered below. However, it should be noted that the rights of live and cadaver donors and the rights of recipients have not been fully spelled out by law at this time. And yet, as already pointed out, there is considerable controversy concerning the desirability of legislative action when a situation is in such flux as is transplantation.

Historical Legal Background

At early common law, neither the deceased nor the surviving spouse nor the next of kin had property rights in the deceased's body. The corpse had no commercial value at common law. That is, it could not be sold. Neither could the dead body be transferred by gift, nor could it be used to satisfy a debt, nor could it be subjected to a lien. Therefore, according to early common law, the only right a live person had over his body, which would someday be a cadaver, was that he might direct the manner and place of his burial in his will. And, these wishes would be legally enforceable if they did not conflict with other prevailing interests (e.g., community religious standards). But, once the body was buried, the law took custody of it, and only a court of equity could authorize its disturbance.

This strict legal doctrine of "no property rights" in a deceased body was later modified by case law in England and in the United States. In the United States, a dead body eventually came to have "quasi-property rights." But these quasi-property rights were strictly defined. Primarily these quasi-property rights in dead bodies consisted of the spouse's or next of kin's right to bury the body, the body custodian's right to sue to recover any damages for mutilation of the dead body, the body custodian's right to grant or withhold permission to perform an autopsy, and the body custodian's right to determine the manner and place of burial.

Surprisingly perhaps, the basic common law concepts of no property rights or quasi-property rights in cadavers still prevail in most American jurisdictions. There have been some modifications by statute or by recent case law as we shall see in the following discussion. But these modifications notwithstanding, it has been argued that the contemporary state of law relating to transplants is archaic and inadequate and that the age of the transplant is crippled by existing law. This will become acutely apparent in the discussion of the legal versus the medical definition of death.

In the sections that follow, we shall deal with general legal propositions applicable to live donors, cadaver donors, and recipients. And finally, we shall briefly consider the physician's malpractice liability for experimentation in vital organ transplants. Finally, we shall consider specific legislation controlling particular aspects of organ transplants in the next chapter on the Uniform Anatomical Gift Act.

Live Donors

The legal questions surrounding live donors are very different from those surrounding cadaver donors. First of all, only certain kinds of transplantation, such as skin grafts or kidney transplants, can utilize live donors. As medical technology exists at the present moment, it is not possible to transplant vital organs other than kidneys when live donors are used. Secondly, it is generally inconceivable to consider a transplant therapeutic from the donor's point of view. The possible exception to the nontherapeutic effect on the donor would be if it can be shown that the donor would so benefit psychologically that his gift of tissue would be therapeutic. Thus, any discussion of legal questions involving a transplant donor will necessarily focus upon the donor's consent.

The fundamental principle of medical jurisprudence--that a patient must consent to any surgical procedure--is extremely important in the case of a live donor. Since he has nothing to gain therapeutically, any removal of tissue can be viewed as experimental vis-a-vis the live donor because he becomes merely a means of adding to the field of medical science in helping to accomplish a transplant in another human being. Hence the donor's consent is the sine qua non of the transplant procedure. We shall first consider the consent of the competent adult donor and then the special class of live donors--minors and incompetents. In order to insure the protection of the hospital and physicians involved in a transplant from tort liability, it is necessary not only to have the donor's express consent, but also his voluntary, informed consent. The donor's voluntary, informed consent can best be manifested by proof of the following: (1) a consent form certifying that the donor was fully cognizant of the transplant procedure as well as its reasonable consequences, and (2) that the transplant donor underwent a psychiatric examination that determined his mental health before the time of the transplant surgery.

Some medical and legal writers maintain that the problem of consent in the case of a competent adult is merely an extension of the consent problem in general. Therefore, according to some medico-legal experts, the mature adult's right to donate any part of his body is included in the broader principle of medical jurisprudence that gives the freedom to choose those medical and surgical procedures to which one is willing to submit. But there are other medical and legal writers who question the rationality of an organ donor's decision. This is due to the fact that most live transplant donors decide to give tissue in a psychologically demanding and highly emotional situation--generally a relative or friend will die without the donated organ. In addition, one must consent to risks other than those involved in the immediate surgery. Namely, the donor must consent to the long-term risk of living without a donated organ.

To date the courts have not considered the legal issue of whether or not a donor's consent to removal of his organ will require higher standards than ordinary informed consent. It is possible that donor consent requirements will be stricter in transplants than in normal medical procedures because of the nontherapeutic physical nature of the organ donation.

Minors and Incompetents

The consent requirement is more complicated where the tissue donor is a minor or incompetent. This is due to the paucity of medical precedent concerning whether a parent, guardian, court, or expert committee may consent for the donor where the surgery is for the sole benefit of another. It has been established that consent is not a prerequisite for normal, general medical treatment where the incompetent or minor will benefit from the medical procedures. But in the nontherapeutic situation of the transplant operation, the physician is certainly on shaky legal ground if he uses a minor or incompetent as a donor. This remains a truism even though in the case of the minor, the donor would be in a far better medical position to undergo the transplant donation than the adult donor.

At common law minors were incapable of consenting to nontherapeutic medical procedures for the benefit of another. And there are no recent cases that hold that minors or incompetents may submit to nontherapeutic surgery on the basis of their own consent. In a 1941 case, Bonner v. Moran, (126 F. 2d 121 (D.C.

Cir. 1941)), a physician was held liable for assault and battery because without proper consent he performed a skin graft on a badly burned boy. The skin donor was the fifteen-year-old cousin of the burned boy. The minor donor gave his consent, but the court held it would have been necessary that the boy's parents also consented. There is some recent judicial authority, however, that gives equity courts the power to authorize the parents or guardians of minor or incompetent tissue donors to consent to organ donation for the infants or incompetents.

Concerning minors, the Massachusetts Supreme Judicial Court has established the following requirements for transplants between minor twins: (1) the minor must be fully informed and understand the consequences of his donation and must consent to the operation; (2) the minor's parents must also consent to the operation; and (3) the transplant must benefit the minor donor in some way (the benefit may be purely psychological).

Likewise, the first appellate court deciding the issue of consent of incompetent tissue donors, arrived at the same conclusion as did the court considering minor tissue donors. In the incompetent donor case, Strunk v. Strunk, (445 S.W. 2d 145 (Ky. Ct. App. 1969)), an incompetent donor was a twenty-seven-year-old with the IQ of a six-year-old. His recipient brother was twenty-eight and was going to die of kidney disease. Since the incompetent brother was the only suitable kidney donor, the brothers' mother petitioned the court for an order allowing a transplant. The petition was granted and affirmed on appeal. The court held that expert psychiatric testimony indicated that the transplantation would be beneficial to the incompetent brother because the death of his brother would have adverse psychological effects.

As a general proposition, then, it seems that courts are willing to authorize transplants involving a minor or incompetent donor as long as such donor derives some benefit from the surgery. If litigation arises in the future wherein it is shown (by expert testimony or otherwise) that a minor or incompetent donor would suffer adverse effects from tissue donation, it is doubtful that the courts could authorize a transplant in view of the evidence of possible detrimental effects on the potential donor.

Cadaver Donors

Since vital organs such as the heart, liver, pancreas, or lungs can be procured only from cadaver donors, legal problems separate from those surrounding live donors arise. The primary legal questions involving deceased donors are: (1) the deceased donor's consent to tissue removal; and (2) defining that point in time when the deceased donor is dead. The concept of the consecration of the human body is entrenched religiously, philosophically, sociologically, and psychologically. Thus the dismantling of the human body has posed grave questions for some time. And the law has devoted statutory attention to the problem of consent to post mortem donations for more than thirty years. Post mortem donation of all or part of the body precedes the transplant age in that medical research and students have needed dead human bodies since the study of anatomy began. Hence the law has reacted to the aged problem of post mortem tissue donation. The law's concern with consent to post mortem tissue donation culminated in the Uniform Anatomical Gift Act, discussed in Chapter VII and set out in Appendix E. We shall here limit our discussion of cadaver donors to the significant and presently unresolved problem of defining death.

Death

Let us assume valid post mortem consent for a human tissue donor and that the donor is on the brink of death. There are then conflicting interests in such a situation. Firstly, the potential donor's attending physician has a duty to extend his patient's life for as long as is possible. Secondly, the transplant surgeon must remove the transplantable organ from the donor as soon as he is deceased. Essentially, the success of the transplant largely depends upon the speed of removal of the healthy organ from the deceased donor. In each case, the physician (attending or transplant) has a primary responsibility to his patient. The situation is a precarious one, for both physicians have a duty to save lives. And, in such a situation either physician could conceivably be influenced by the proposed use of the virtually dead donor's organ to relax the traditional standards for determining death.

But, relaxation of the standard for pronouncing death is but one aspect of the controversy surrounding death and transplants. The basic more difficult problem is arriving at a legal definition of death that truly reflects the modern medical definition of death. Transplant surgeons justifiably desire a legal redefinition of death.

There are several difficulties of applying the present legal definition of death to the transplant situation. Of the more noticeable difficulties, one problem is that court decisions explicitly defining death in connection with a transplant are nonexistent.

Most cases that have defined death have centered around the issue of survivorship to property. As a spin-off issue of death in the context of property succession, the courts have inherited a tradition of giving weight to lay testimony in determining the moment of death. There is therefore a tendency in the law to look to nonexpert testimony involving the issue of death in spite of the wealth of medical opinion and scientific knowledge. Basically, then, medical opinion concerning the definition of death is still limited by archaic legal definition. And that legal definition is entrenched because the courts have been dealing with questions of property and survivorship for generations. Therefore the attending physician has the responsibility of certifying a patient's death by the legal rather than the medical definition thereof.

What then are the legal and medical definitions of death? The legal definition is simplistic considering contemporary medical knowledge. The law still defines death as "a total stoppage of the circulation of the blood, and a cessation of the animal and vital functions consequent thereon." In other words the legal definition centers around the cessation of the heartbeat. However, we really need not browbeat the legal profession for its outmoded definition of death. For until the transplant era, death was merely medically recognized and a detailed definition was unnecessary. As a matter of fact the superannuated legal definition is the adopted medical definition of past decades.

It is, therefore, only recently that the medical profession revised its criterion for determining death from a cessation of heartbeat to a "brain death" focus. A revision of the medical definition of death was necessitated by the modern biomedical advances enabling physicians to control vital organ functions by machines. Thus a patient's heartbeat and respiration may appear normal even though he no longer has control of these vital organ functions. Consequently the medical profession was forced to reexamine its heartbeat definition of death. Medical workers discovered that death involves neurological impairment manifested by the nonfunctioning of the brain and irreversible coma.

Dr. Henry Beecher and the Harvard Medical School have studied the permanent nonfunctioning of the brain and have developed the so-called "Harvard Criteria" to be used in determining brain death. The criteria are: (1) deep unconciousness and no response to external needs; (2) absence of movement and breathing; (3) lack of body reflexes; and (4) a flat or isoclectric electroencephalogram made twenty-four hours apart serving as confirmatory evidence of death.

The task of changing the judicial definition of death in view of present and ever changing advances is dual-faceted. As a starting point, the old "heartbeat cessation" definition of death should be totally eliminated from the judicial outlook on death. And a new orientation needs to be adopted. Death should be defined by medical experts who can keep pace with medical knowledge and technology. State legislatures have not set up statutory definitions of death and the Uniform Anatomical Gift Act does not address itself to an explicit definition of death. This was undoubtedly intentional since any definition of death risks being acceptable only at the time of the definition, as new medical knowledge may change it. Perhaps the legal profession should invest time in determining how many medical experts should pronounce death and under what circumstances they may do so, without seeking express criteria for legally defining death. The greater the flexibility for encompassing future medical and scientific progress in whatever legal controls are set forth in the transplant situation, the more sensible the judicial result.

Recipients

The medical and legal problems involving an organ transplant recipient are as complex as those involving an organ transplant donor. The only mitigating factor lessening the potential malpractice liability of a transplanting physician is that a transplant should be in the direct therapeutic interests of the recipient unless performed for nontherapeutic reasons. The onus of responsibility for the legal (as well as medical) decision falls upon the transplant physician. The problems to which a transplant physician must address himself are whether to perform the transplant, how to find a suitable organ donor within approved procedures therefor, and obtaining valid consent from the organ recipient.

The key question for the transplant physician is whether to perform the transplant at all. The surgeon must attempt to judge whether the transplant recipient will live longer with or without surgery. In his attempt to decide this preliminary question the physician must consider whether the recipient has a good chance of surviving transplant surgery and the possibilities of tissue rejection. In the final analysis, the transplant physician's own judgment must prevail because it is virtually impossible to prove whether a patient would have lived without the transplant. Therefore, the physician's decision as to whether or not to perform is a vital one that he must be prepared to defend by showing he knowledgably exercised that degree of care and skill ordinarily possessed and exercised by other members of the medical profession. If he is unable to defend his decision, he may be held liable for malpractice, particularly since the transplant is still considered experimental surgery by many.

Once the transplant physician has decided to perform the surgery, he must then obtain the appropriate consent of the recipient (or his parent or guardian if the recipient is a minor or incompetent). In order to stave off future tort liability, the organ recipient as well as the organ donor must consent to the transplant operation. The recipient's consent should be consistent with the doctrine of informed consent, which the courts will undoubtedly strictly apply in transplant litigation stemming from injuries to the recipient. The informed consent requires in this instance that the recipient be informed of (1) all risks inherent in the transplant operation; (2) the possibility of tissue rejection and its endangerment of the recipient's life even if the transplant is performed; and (3) any possible alternative methods of treatment of the illness.

In addition, it is strongly recommended that once the transplant recipient has been informed of all foreseeable risks involved in a transplant operation, a physician other than the immediate transplant surgeon obtain the recipient's consent. The transplant surgeon's delegation of this duty would protect him against future charges that he exerted undue influence in obtaining the recipient's consent so that he might outperform his colleagues in the number of transplants completed.

But, even if the recipient does consent, the transplant physician must continue his decision-making process into a final stage; he must find a suitable tissue donor. If he chooses an unsuitable donor, he may be liable for malpractice on the basis of suitability of donors. The dangers of utilizing organs from unsuitable donors lie in tissue rejection. Therefore, the transplant physician must match tissue structure and blood types between donor and recipient. He must also consider the age differential between donor and recipient as well as the size difference between the donated organ and the diseased one. Due to the relative novelty of organ transplants, the medical profession has not established standards for suitable donors. Therefore, if litigation arises concerning the question of suitable donors, the courts will most certainly have to rely on expert testimony from facts gained from previous organ transplants.

Physician's Liability for Transplant Experimentation

Thus we see that a physician may be held liable for medical malpractice in connection with transplantation of tissue and possibly for experimentation in connection with vital organ transplants. Although the potential for criminal liability exists, if the transplant is therapeutic, it is unlikely that a district attorney would prosecute. We shall therefore reiterate the areas in which a transplant physician may be charged with civil liability. Then we shall consider how a judicial decision could hinge upon experimentation rather than medical malpractice.

The bases of civil liability of a transplant surgeon include the following: (1) failure to obtain informed consent of an adult organ donor or recipient; (2) failure to obtain the consent of a minor or incompetent organ recipient's parent or guardian; (3) failure to obtain court authorization for a minor or incompetent organ donation; (4) failure to use the organ of a "suitable" donor; (5) faulty judgment in the decision to perform the transplantation; (6) negligence in performing the transplant surgery; and (7) negligence in preoperative or postoperative transplant procedures and treatment. In addition, the physician attending a potential deceased donor could be held civilly liable (or criminally liable, for that matter) in negligently or overzealously certifying the donor's death prematurely.

Since courts are wont to avoid the issue of human experimentation per se, any transplant litigation may be framed in terms of medical malpractice. However, the therapeutic transplant litigation* could be properly based on human experimentation for any of the following reasons: (1) it is presently impossible to positively control tissue rejection; (2) there are divergent opinions concerning postoperative treatment of vital organ transplant recipients; (3) the use of human beings in transplanting vital organs is still recent; (4) accepted medical standards for determining suitable tissue donors are nonexistent; and (6) the transplant recipient's death is certain if faulty medical judgment is acted upon.

To summarize then, elements of human experimentation

---

*Obviously nontherapeutic transplant litigation should be based on experimentation, if the issue arises.

presently exist in the area of vital organ transplants. Even with the vast increase in the number of vital organ transplants, that, in itself, will not reduce the physician's potential liability for experimentation. Before the potential liability can be removed, the transplant will have to be a universally accepted method of medical treatment and medically accepted standards will have to be issued.

Chapter 7

THE UNIFORM ANATOMICAL GIFT ACT

As pointed out in the previous chapter on transplantation, the renewed concern in property rights in and the disposition of the dead human body, has been spurred by the rather recent public awareness and interest in heart transplants. The medical progress enabling the heart transplant quickly provided the incentive for drafting and enacting new legislation dealing with post mortem tissue donation because the existing law was inadequate and confusing. The onslaught of publicity by the news media spawned enough public interest in the practical means whereby human bodies and parts thereof could be distributed to the living to prompt the National Conference on Uniform Laws to draft the Uniform Anatomical Gift Act (hereinafter referred to as the U.A.G.A.; see Appendix E for the text of the act).

The author has chosen to treat the U.A.G.A. separately from the general subject of transplantation for the following reasons: (1) the U.A.G.A. is an example of uniform legislation that can be adopted by all state jurisdictions; it is thus a possible model for regulating other aspects of human experimentation; (2) the U.A.G.A. is a flexible statute in that it makes room for further advances in medical progress and scientific technology and it therefore contradicts some of the criticisms leveled by those who consider attempts to regulate human experimentation by statute ill-advised; and (3) the U.A.G.A. is tangible proof that the law can and should respond when there is immediate and direct need for it to do so.

The Pre-U.A.G.A. Legal Condition

Prior to the U.A.G.A., many states had statutes dealing with at least some aspects of the disposition of dead bodies. Those states that totally lacked statutes were in a helpless state of affairs in that the existing common law was extremely confusing as to the various rights and interests in the dead human body and its parts. However, before the adoption of the U.A.G.A. those forty-two states, in addition to the District of Columbia, that did have some form of legislation permitting post mortem tissue donation to science lacked uniformity. The unquestionable conclusion of most authorities was that the diversity and confusion in the statutory law as well as the common law resulted in a completely inadequate system of legal control of matters relating to organ transplantation. In response to these legal inadequacies, the Commissioners on Uniform State Laws established a special committee to draft a uniform donation statute. The special committee was created in 1965. In July, 1968, the U.A.G.A. was approved by the National Conference on Uniform Laws and by the American Bar Association.

State Adoption of the U.A.G.A.

All fifty states and the District of Columbia had adopted the U.A.G.A. in some form by the end of 1971. The U.A.G.A. was intended to be a model donation statute that would remove the major legal problems created by outdated and widely varying laws. In addition to the U.A.G.A.'s anticipated correction of lack of uniformity in the various state statutes, it was hoped that the adoption of the act would also alleviate the legal problems inherent in a highly mobile American society where peripatetic citizens constantly travel from state to state. For example, a hypothetical problem could arise where Ms. Donor had executed an ante mortem tissue gift to Charity Hospital which was located in Iowa, but died in a traffic accident in Nebraska. The uniform adoption of the U.A.G.A. was intended to ameliorate the medical problem of removal of an organ at the critical time as well as the attendant problem of legal liability for removing the organ outside the state of donation where the donor did not die in the state of donation. And as an extension of the above explicit example, the U.A.G.A. was drafted with the purpose of allowing the donated tissues to be used in Maine or New York or Washington. That is, the ultimate goal of the U.A.G.A. was to facilitate the removal of the donated tissues as well as their transportation to their most socially useful ends.

As previously discussed, states may adopt varying statutes in exercising the powers reserved to the states. Therefore, no state was compelled to adopt the statute as promulgated by the National Conference on Uniform Laws. Nonetheless, adoption by the various states of the U.A.G.A. has resulted in a great deal of uniformity in state legislation. Section 3 of the act, which treats the questions of which persons may become donees and the purposes for which anatomical gifts may be made, has been the most uniformly adopted. Most state acts consider hospitals, physicians, teaching institutions, storage banks, and specified individuals as donees. And the purposes of the donations of bodies or parts thereof that are included in state statutes usually include transplantation, therapy, teaching, and research.

Section 4 of the act, which deals with the manner of executing anatomical gifts, has also been adopted with great uniformity by the states. Anatomical gifts may be executed by will, in which case such gifts become effective immediately upon the donor's death without waiting for the will to be probated. Therefore, even if the gift is subsequently deemed invalid, the gift is nevertheless effective to the extent it has been acted upon. Section 4 also provides that the anatomical gift may be made by any other properly signed document (e.g., the Uniform Donor Card; see Appendix F). The Uniform Donor Card is very helpful in that the donor carries it with him, thereby insuring that his wishes are implemented in case he is involved in an accident.

Purposes of the U.A.G.A.

The U.A.G.A.'s purpose is to provide comprehensive answers to questions involving the gift of all or parts of a human body. It supplies answers to the following questions. By whom may a gift of parts of the body be made? To whom may a gift be made? What are the provisions for revocation of the gift? What is the effect of the donor's gift on the rights of surviving relatives? What is the effect of the donor's gift on the civil and criminal liability of the surgeon and other medical personnel participating in the removal of the parts? The primary answers to the above questions follow.

Any individual of sound mind who is over eighteen years of age may donate all or any part of his body. In addition, the act provides that the surviving kin may execute a donation of the decendent's body or any part thereof unless there is (1) actual notice of decendent's contrary intent or (2) opposition by a member of the same or a prior (that is, superior) class as the surviving kin attempting the execution. The effect of the surviving kin donation provision is to authorize a parent or other survivor of a deceased minor to execute an anatomical gift although the minor would have been unable to execute the gift himself.

As stated above in the discussion of "State Adoption of the U.A.G.A.," the act includes hospitals, physicians, teaching institutions, storage banks, and specified individuals as proper recipients of anatomical gifts.

The act provides for the revocation of an anatomical gift by will or other instrument. A gift may be revoked by a signed writing, an oral statement witnessed by two persons, a signed donor's card found on the donor or with his effects, or by a statement to an attending physician made during a terminal illness. Any anatomical gift may also be amended by any of the methods outlined above.

The act also provides the answer to the question of the rights of the surviving relatives of the donor. It states that after the removal of the donated part or parts, the surviving spouse, the next of kin, or those charged with the disposal of the donor's body are given custody of the remainder of the donor's body.

Finally, the act sets forth an explicit answer to the important question of the legal liability of medical persons involved in the transplant situation. Section 7 (c) states: "A person who acts in good faith in accord with the terms of this Act or the anatomical gift laws of another State (or a foreign country) is not liable for damages in any civil action or subject to prosecution in any criminal proceeding for his act." In short, a physician or other person who acts in good faith and within the U.A.G.A.'s provisions will not be subject to any civil action or criminal prosecution. Clearly, the purpose of the provision is to negative the civil and criminal liability of physicians and surgeons in the transplant situation. However, the good faith requirement of the provision militates against the exculpating of a negligent physician or surgeon from a valid claim of medical malpractice when the physician is involved in the medical treatment of a donor patient.

Unanswered Questions

In the first place, the U.A.G.A. does not answer the question of who the recipient of donated parts shall be in the event that the demand for such parts is greater than the supply thereof.

Secondly, the act does not define when viable organs may be removed from the donor body for transplant purposes. In other words, the U.A.G.A. does not attempt to define the moment of death. It provides that the treating physician determine the time of death of the donor. Although the act's omission of a definition of death may cause concern in some quarters, it can be viewed as an attempt to build flexibility into the act by leaving room for perpetual redefinition of death in accordance with medical and scientific advancements.

Conclusion

There continues to be a growing number of organ and tissue transplants performed yearly. In fact, some tissue and organ transplants are becoming commonplace. Considering the increase in transplants, there are very few decisions involving the Uniform Anatomical Gift Act. This relative paucity of litigation has been encouraging. It points to the conclusion that the U.A.G.A. is an effective legal device that has solved at least one small segment of one area of human experimentation.

In view of the apparent success of the act and its overwhelming acceptance and uniform adoption by all the states and the District of Columbia, a further possibility presents itself. The federal government should consider the adoption of a law similar to the U.A.G.A. as well as supporting legislation for the main law. Were the federal government to do so, the flow of organs and tissues from state to state would be protected. This would operate to further decrease the conflicts of law among the states. The United States Congress has ample authority to regulate the matter under its power over interstate commerce under Article I, section 8 of the United States Constitution. This constitutional authority has been the base of much federal legislation in areas that would normally be the province of the states.

Chapter 8

PSYCHOLOGICAL EXPERIMENTATION

The modern psychological treatment of mental disorders in Western cultures was primarily derived from the attempts by Sigmund Freud and Josef Breuer toward the end of the nineteenth century to devise a "talking cure" for psychological illnesses. The conventional means for effecting the Freud-Breuer derived "talking cure" have been psychoanalysis, individual psychotherapy, various forms of group therapy, and environment therapy. The definitions of the foregoing terms follow.

Psychoanalysis is a method of psychotherapy, originated by Sigmund Freud, designed to bring preconscious and unconscious material to consciousness and carried out largely through the analysis of transference and resistance. Individual psychotherapy **is the treatment of mental disease based primarily upon verbal** or nonverbal communication between the patient and his therapist. Group therapy is the treatment of mental disease based upon verbal or nonverbal communication in which two or more patients participate with their therapist. Environment therapy or "milieu therapy" is psychiatric treatment consisting of providing the patient with an environment that is expected to influence his condition in a beneficial manner, e.g., day hospital. All the conventional "talking cures" depend upon contact and some form of communication between the patient/client and therapist.

In the typical situation there is an unbalance between the client's perceived self and his actual experiences. The therapist's optimal reaction is one of congruence in which he provides accurate perceptions of the therapist-client relationship and reacts with unconditional favorable regard toward the client. The client then perceives the therapist's regard and understanding, which results in personality changes in the client. The important feature of the above approaches is that they are all client-centered and require the client's participation in order to modify behavior.

During the past four decades or so these conventional methods of psychological treatment have been supplemented or replaced by somatic (also called physical or organic) methods of treatment. Such somatic methods do not require the client's participation or cooperation; they are often administered against his will. To be sure somatic treatment of mental disorders is not a new concept. Alcmaeon and Hippocrates asserted the somatic nature of mental illnesses more than two thousand years ago. Somatic procedures used to treat mental illness through the centuries include solitary confinement, bloodletting, whipping, pouring ice water and even scalding water on patients, and castration, as well as superstitious rituals such as drinking concoctions made of blood and amphibians, etc. Somatic methods of treating mental disorders were popular through the nineteenth century because they were the only known methods. The subsequent twentieth-century theories, enabling a therapeutic attack of mental problems, only came about due to the clinically valid classification of mental diseases by Kraepelin and the introduction of the principles of psychodynamic theory by Freud.

It was not until approximately 1930 that the interest in the somatic treatment of mental illness was reawakened. The renewed interest was probably given its main impetus by the reported experiments of Loevenhart et al in 1929. These experiments alleged that the injection of small quantities of potassium cyanate coupled with the inhalation of carbon dioxide in mute and motionless patients resulted in the patients' abilities to talk and move again while they were under the influence of these drugs. Today the major forms of somatic treatment of mental illness are psychopharmacology, shock therapy, and psychosurgery. The definitions of the foregoing terms follow.

Psychopharmacology is the use of drugs to influence affective and emotional states. Shock therapy is the production of convulsions by the administration of insulin, pentylenetetrazol, etc., or by an electric current passed through the head; it is used in the treatment of certain mental disorders. Psychosurgery is the treatment of mental disorders by operation upon the brain, e.g., lobotomy. Use of any of the above organic methods for treating mental disorders carries the inherent risk of adversely affecting the patient. For example, the extended use of tranquilizing or neuroleptic drugs can cause nervous disorders; electroshock treatment may cause fractured or broken bones; psychosurgery destroys irreplaceable brain cells and tissues.

It follows then that although persons should have no rational basis for opposing the "talking cure" or psychodynamic methods of psychotherapy, the same cannot be said of somatic methods of treatment of psychological disorders. These somatic methods may be classified as types of behavior control. In the classical approach to behavior control the therapist has paired the patient's undesirable behavior with an electric shock or an emetic drug. The classical approach has been used to treat homosexual fixation, drug addiction, and all kinds of sexual deviance. Although such behavior control has been familiar to psychiatrists for some time, it is only recently that the subject has been brought to the legal profession's attention due to its widespread use in national institutions, e.g., prisons.

In the discussion that follows, we shall limit ourselves to enforced somatic behavior control therapy and the legal questions presented thereby. We shall first briefly examine the experimental nature of somatic behavior control therapy. Secondly we shall look at the legal considerations relevant to enforced somatic behavior control therapy. And finally we shall individually examine the three representative types of somatic behavior control therapy (psychopharmacology, shock therapy, and psychosurgery) outlined above in order to apply some legal considerations inherent in each type of somatic behavior control therapy.

Experimental Nature of Somatic Behavior Control Therapy

Somatic treatment of mental disorders is therapeutic for psychosis whereas some form of psychotherapy is generally considered therapeutic in the treatment of psychoneuroses. Although it is generally accepted that the somatic treatment of psychotic illness is effective in many cases, the same physical methods are of limited value for successfully treating neurotic disorders. Yet in spite of its effectiveness and notwithstanding the fact that drugs, shock treatment procedures, and psychosurgery may have been "sufficiently tested" methods for treating psychological disorders, somatic treatment of mental illness may be considered prima facie experimental. The study of psychological phenomena is still considered an inexact science by many medical professionals. The exact relationship between the physical and mental nature of man is still undetermined and there appears to be a growing uneasiness in the medical profession concerning the insufficient medical knowledge of the brain and its functions.

But the ultimate results of such techniques--whether somatic or psychotherapeutic--cannot be measured in advance. That is not to say that the treatment of psychological disorders is unlike the treatment of exclusively physical disorders. Even in the treatment of physical disorders, the effectiveness of a particular cure is dependent upon the patient's individual response thereto. However, the main difference between the treatment of psychological and physiological disorders is that in the treatment of psychological disorders the end result is based upon intuitive observations of the administering therapist. There is no objective measuring stick (e.g., electrocardiogram) for indicating the range of normalcy in the treatment of many psychological illnesses. This is due to the fact that there is no universally agreed-upon definition of psychological normalcy among psychologists, psychiatrists, or lay persons. In short then, the treatment of mental disorders is still experimental by its very nature.

Furthermore we are dealing with the enforced somatic treatment of mental disorders which is ordinarily applied to prisoners and mental patients. The public has recently turned its attention to general conditions in prisons and mental institutions (particularly those mental institutions that are state funded) in which experiments <u>qua</u> experiments are conducted upon the persons therein. The contention that psychological experimentation within the human experimentation definition is conducted in the institutionalized setting is based upon two premises. Firstly and generally, the nature of psychological "healing" is still experimental in a cause and effect sense. Secondly and specifically, <u>actual</u> experimentation is conducted upon criminals and other institutionalized persons as a form of behavior control therapy with great frequency. Based upon the foregoing we shall now probe the legal ramifications of coerced psychological experimentation.

Legal Considerations

The primary legal consideration involved in the question of coerced somatic psychological therapy is the abridgment of the individual's constitutional rights. The constitutional rights that are infringed upon are those protected by the First, Fourth, Eighth, Ninth, and Fourteenth Amendments to the United States Constitution.

First Amendment Rights. The First Amendment protects communication and the generation of ideas. Therefore coerced somatic therapy, which inhibits a person's ability to express himself, is a direct invasion of the First Amendment.

Fourth Amendment Rights. The Fourth Amendment guarantees the individual's right of personal privacy and dignity. Fourth Amendment limitations upon the power of the state to intrude upon the individual's privacy include the forced intrusion of the integrity of the mind as well as the body. Thus the administering of psychotherapeutic drugs or shock as well as the performance of psychosurgery invade the protection afforded by the Fourth Amendment on two counts. First, the right to body integrity is abridged by all the procedures. Secondly, the administering of any of the somatic treatments ipso facto invades the mental integrity of the individual by producing a change in the individual's mental state.

Eighth Amendment Rights. The Eighth Amendment bans "cruel and unusual punishment." Therefore one can object to a particular form of therapy or to the way it is administered. The counterargument that coerced somatic therapy is not a violation of one's Eighth Amendment right centers upon the definition of punishment. Proponents of the use of coerced somatic therapy refuse to obliterate the distinction between "punishment" and "treatment." However, it is difficult to lend credence to a distinction between the two terms when dealing with the incarceration situation of prisoners or state mental patients. In its clearest terms, then, the cruel and unusual punishment clause of the Eighth Amendment requires respect for human dignity and any treatment that violates that dignity may be considered cruel and unusual punishment. In that context, treatment and cruel and unusual punishment may become synonymous.

Ninth Amendment Rights. The Ninth Amendment may be said to apply to the enforced therapy situation. The Ninth Amendment protects those basic rights that are not specifically enumerated in the other amendments to the Constitution. Included under the Ninth Amendment is the right of the individual to retain his personality inviolate. This right to the protection of one's personality encompasses freedom of thought and emotion. Obviously, any sort of enforced somatic therapy precludes the retention of the private personality intact.

Fourteenth Amendment Rights. Section 1 of the Fourteenth Amendment to the Constitution reads: "All persons born or naturalized in the United States, and subject to the jurisdiction thereof, are citizens of the United States and of the State wherein they reside. No State shall make or enforce any law which shall abridge the privileges or immunities of citizens of the United States; nor shall any State deprive any person of life, liberty, or property, without due process of law; nor deny to any person within its jurisdiction the equal protection of the laws."

Coerced somatic therapy may be attacked as an infringement of both the due process and equal protection clauses of the Fourteenth Amendment. The due process clause may be invoked in the enforced therapy situation whenever a patient or prisoner is forced to submit to any unwanted therapeutic method or procedure. The protection of every individual's liberty is the purpose of procedural due process and any violation or abridgment of the individual's rights is an attack upon the due process clause of the Constitution.

Although courts have been slow to act upon questions presented by enforced treatment of prisoners and mental patients based upon the equal protection clause of the Fourteenth Amendment, the clause nevertheless provides a strong argument for the attack on coerced treatment. The legal argument focused upon the equal protection clause involves whether or not the detection and treatment of a prisoner or patient for an alleged mental disorder, absent the use of the same procedures for detecting and treating mental disorders of any other group, is a violation of equal protection of the prisoner or the patient. Simply stated, the question of equal protection is posed where there is differential treatment among groups of people. The courts' reluctance to act on the basis of equal protection is due to the presumption that the institutional personnel charged with the treatment of prisoners and patients are able to classify differentially such individuals and to determine the appropriateness of their treatment.

Legal Consent

The obvious problem with the consent of a prisoner or mental patient to somatic psychological therapy is the ability of such individuals to give valid consent. Before the drastic methods of somatic treatment are considered, the patient's mental condition is presumably psychotic and thus incompetent. If the patient has been legally adjudicated incompetent, he is legally incapable of giving his consent. It is unclear however whether or not a patient who has not been legally deemed incompetent may technically consent by having his judgment substituted by the state under the state's power of parens patriae (the sovereign power of guardianship over persons under disability).

In addition to the question of a patient's competency to consent to somatic psychological therapy, there is the second question of the patient's awareness. That is, in addition to his manifestation of a willingness to undergo a method of treatment (consent) is his consent "informed" in the sense that he is aware of the risks and consequences of his consent to the proposed treatment? Therefore, informed consent includes the therapist's duty to provide the patient with the information necessary for the patient to make a rational decision concerning the proposed method of therapy.

The real problem with consent in the context of an involuntarily detained prisoner or mental patient is the voluntariness of consent. And the problem is threefold. First, is the person competent to give consent? Secondly, is he aware of all the ramifications of that consent? Thirdly, is the environment in which he exists so inherently coercive and do his privileges so depend upon his cooperation that he is unable to withhold his consent for fear of reprisal by the institutional administrators?

The other consideration involved in consent by the patient to undergo somatic treatment concerns the situation wherein it is truly impossible for the patient to give competent and informed consent. That is undoubtedly the general case when dealing with a population of prisoners or mental patients. Is third party consent valid? The third party may be a parent or guardian or the state. Courts usually attempt to objectively balance the risks to the patient against the welfare of the individual and the general societal welfare in testing the validity of third party consent. Although there are often too many motivational factors involved in third party consent (e.g., a parent's unwillingness to deal with his offspring's aberrant behavior or an institution's interest in being able to manage a given patient), courts nonetheless generally permit third party consent as an alternative to the individual patient's consent.

Ideally, the courts should establish an objective standard on which to base constructive consent, thus substituting judicial opinion for third party consent. This solution, too, presents complications in that the medical expertise may not be available to the judicial decision makers. Moreover, it is of questionable practicality due to the additional financial burden it would place upon the courts and due to the impossibility of deciding such cases within a time frame that would be beneficial to the patient. It would be disastrous to withhold consent to a given type of somatic therapy (assuming that such therapy is ever beneficial) while the case remained in the limbo of the regular overcrowded, unmanageable court docket.

We shall now turn to the discussion of psychopharmacology, shock therapy, and psychosurgery. Under each method of somatic treatment we shall examine a court case testing the method in order to better understand the legal problems inherent in each method of treatment.

Psychopharmacology

In Mackey v. Procunier, (477 F.2d 877 (9th Cir. 1973)), Mackey, a state prisoner, brought suit against defendants alleging cruel and unusual punishment. Mackey had consented to undergo shock treatment at a state medical facility where the staff was engaged in medical and psychiatric experimentation with "aversive treatment" of criminal offenders. But without his consent, he was administered succinycholine, a "fright drug." Plaintiff alleged that as a result of the drug he regularly suffers nightmares in which he experiences great fright and awakens unable to breathe. The drug is one recommended as an adjunct to electric-shock therapy as a relaxant. But it should not be administered to fully conscious patients due to its frightening effects. The appellate court held that the prisoner's complaint, alleging that he had received a "fright drug" without consent, sufficiently alleged cruel and unusual punishment. It further found that the forcible injection of an experimental drug into a prisoner constituted "impermissible tinkering with the mental processes."

Shock Therapy

In New York City Health and Hospitals Corporation v. Stein, (70 Misc. 2d 944, 335 N.Y.S. 2d 461 (1972)), the corporation applied to the court for an order authorizing the psychiatric staff of Bellevue Hospital to administer electroshock therapy to the respondent-patient, Paula Stein. Stein objected to the shock treatment and refused to consent to it. Although she had undergone two electroshock treatments, the Mental Hygiene Law was recodified thereafter. It required the patient's consent. Thus, the petitioners petitioned the court to issue an order overriding Stein's refusal to consent. The court considered conflicting testimony of psychiatrists concerning the desirability of electroshock treatment for respondent. It held that evidence established that the patient suffered from chronic schizophrenia with tendencies for acute flare-ups and assertedly required psychiatric treatment within a structured environment. However, the court found that although the patient was sufficiently ill to require further retention, she had the mental capacity to know and understand whether or not she wished to consent to electroshock therapy. It therefore denied the application to continue the electroshock therapy.

Psychosurgery

Kaimowitz v. Department of Mental Health, (Civil No. 73-19434-AW (Cir. Ct. Wayne County, Mich., July 10, 1973)) is the only known case dealing with psychosurgery even though such surgery has been performed on more than 50,000 American mental patients during the past thirty years.

The facts of the case follow. In 1972 the director of the Department of Mental Health asked John Doe, a thirty-six-year-old mental patient at Michigan's Ionia State Hospital, to participate in a state-funded experiment. The experiment was designed to test two methods of reducing aggression in chronically violent mental patients. One method involved the administration of a drug and the other involved the psychosurgical destruction of areas of the brain. John Doe had been civilly committed to the care of the Department of Mental Health when he was eighteen; he was considered a sexual psychopath. He gave signed consent to participate in the psychosurgery treatment group. His parents also gave their written permission for the experiment. However, Michigan Legal Services attorney Gabe Kaimowitz brought suit to enjoin the state from performing psychosurgery on John Doe or any other similarly situated person. The court appointed counsel to represent Doe's interests because Doe continued to demonstrate an interest in receiving the experimental treatment. However, in March of 1973, the Wayne County Circuit Court granted Doe his freedom, holding that the research project was a violation of the equal protection clause of the Constitution.

The state withdrew funds for the experiment but the court nevertheless continued to hear arguments and expert testimony about the brain during the spring of 1973. The court reasoned that Kaimowitz represented the class of Michigan mental patients potentially subject to psychosurgical experimentation even though John Doe was technically free. The court then ruled as follows: (1) patients involuntarily committed in state institutions are incapable of giving legally competent, voluntary, and knowledgeable consent to experimental psychosurgical operations; (2) psychosurgery violated the First Amendment rights of freedom of speech and expression which presuppose the right to generate ideas, which could be destroyed by the psychosurgical operation; (3) the medical intrusion into the patient's brain that is presented by psychosurgery abridges the patient's constitutional right to privacy.

The Kaimowitz decision is very important vis-a-vis the law's attempt to regulate man's recent power to control behavior.

It deals with the patient's incompetence to consent to psychosurgery as well as the severity of the psychosurgery itself. The case represents a departure from the familiar approach of analyzing somatic treatment of mental disorders from the point of view of the informed consent doctrine. The case therefore answers some of the issues posed by psychosurgery performed on detained populations.

Conclusion

There seems to be a growing trend in the legal community to react to the behavior control of detained populations with great caution. There seems to be a strengthening awareness that the health and life of persons suffering from mental disorders should receive primary consideration and that the state must have a very compelling interest to outweigh the patient's individual interest. The courts have recently taken cognizance of the fact that there is great controversy among the members of the psychiatric profession concerning the efficacy and the dangers inherent in the somatic treatment of psychological illnesses. Legislators on a state and national level are increasingly aware of the problems of somatic treatment of mental disorders. The U.S. Senate Committee on Labor and Public Welfare (Subcommittee on Health) entertained much discussion of psychosurgery in its hearings on the quality of health care during the Ninety-third Congress in 1973. It is likely that state and national legislators will continue their efforts to control psychological experimentation upon detained populations by enacting legislation.

APPENDICES

Appendix A

EUGENIC STERILIZATION STATUTES

The states that have statutes permitting compulsory sterilization follow. The name of the state is followed by the citation to its pertinent statute. Appendix B contains the text of the Connecticut law dealing with compulsory sterilization.

ALABAMA	ALA. CODE tit. 45, § 243 (1959)
CALIFORNIA	CAL. WELF. & INST'NS CODE § 7254 (Supp. 1974)
CONNECTICUT	CONN. GEN. STAT. REV. § 17-19 (Supp. 1974-75)
DELAWARE	DEL. CODE ANN. tit. 16, §§ 5701-5705 (1953)
GEORGIA	GA. CODE ANN. § 84-933 (Supp. 1974)
INDIANA	IND. ANN. STAT. § 22-1608 (1964)
IOWA	IOWA CODE ANN. § 145.9 (1972)
MAINE	ME. REV. STAT. ANN. tit. 34, § 2461 (1964)
MICHIGAN	MICH. STAT. ANN. §§ 14-381-82 (1969)
MINNESOTA	MINN. STAT. ANN. § 256.07-.08 (1971)
MISSISSIPPI	MISS. CODE ANN. § 6957 (1952)
NEW HAMPSHIRE	N.H. REV. STAT. ANN. § 174:1 (Supp. 1973)
NORTH CAROLINA	N.C. GEN. STAT. § 35-36 (Supp. 1974)
OKLAHOMA	OKLA. STAT. tit. 43a, §§ 341-46 (1961)
OREGON	ORE. REV. STAT. § 436.070 (1965)
SOUTH CAROLINA	S.C. CODE ANN. §§ 32-671-80 (1962)
UTAH	UTAH CODE ANN. § 64-10-1-14 (1953)
VIRGINIA	VA. CODE ANN. § 37.1-171.1 (Supp. 1974)
WISCONSIN	WIS. STAT. ANN. § 46.12 (1967)

Appendix B

CONNECTICUT GENERAL STATUTES § 17-19
(ADOPTED 1969)

17-19. Operations to prevent procreation permitted in training schools

The superintendent of the Mansfield Training School and the superintendent of The Southbury Training School are authorized and directed to appoint for each of said institutions two skilled surgeons, who, in conjunction with the physician or surgeon in charge at each of said institutions, shall constitute a board the duty of which shall be to examine such patients of said institutions as are reported to them, by the superintendent or the physician or surgeon in charge, to be persons by whom procreation would be inadvisable. Such board shall examine the physical and mental conditions of such persons, and if, in the judgment of a majority of such board, procreation by any such person would be inadvisable because he is incapable of comprehending the consequences of his actions, the superintendent of the institution shall make application to the probate court in the district wherein such institution is located for consent for such board to appoint one of its members to perform the operation of vasectomy or tubal surgery, as the case may be, upon such person. Such operations shall be performed in a safe and humane manner, and shall be performed only with the written consent of the responsible next of kin or guardian of the person involved or, if there is none, with the approval of the board of trustees of the institution. The board making such examination and the surgeon performing such operation shall receive from the state such compensation for services rendered as the superintendent of either of said schools deems reasonable.

Appendix C

STATE STATUTES PROHIBITING OR LIMITING FETAL EXPERIMENTATION

The states that have statutes limiting or prohibiting fetal experimentation follow. The name of the state is followed by the citation to its pertinent statute. Appendix C contains the text of the Massachusetts law dealing with fetal experimentation.

CALIFORNIA	CAL. HEALTH & SAFETY CODE § 25956 (West Supp. 1974)
ILLINOIS	Pub. Act No. 78-225, § 8 (July 19, 1973), [1973] Ill. Laws--
INDIANA	IND. CODE § 35-1-58.5-6 (Supp. 1974)
LOUISIANA	LA. REV. STAT. ANN. § 14:87.2 (Supp. 1974)
MAINE	ME. REV. STAT. ANN. tit. 22, § 1574 (Supp. 1973)
MASSACHUSETTS	MASS. GEN. LAWS ANN. ch. 112, § 12J (1975)
MINNESOTA	MINN. STAT. ANN. § 145.422 (Supp. 1974)
NEBRASKA	NEB. REV. STAT. § 28-4, 161 (Supp. 1973)
SOUTH DAKOTA	S.D. COMPILED LAWS ANN. § 34-23A-17 (Supp. 1974)
UTAH	UTAH CODE ANN. § 76-7-312 (Supp. 1973)

Appendix D

MASSACHUSETTS GENERAL LAWS, ch. 112, § 12 J
(ADOPTED JUNE 26, 1974)

No person shall use any live human fetus, whether before or after expulsion from its mother's womb, for scientific, laboratory, research or other kind of experimentation. This section shall not prohibit procedures incident to the study of a human fetus while it is in its mother's womb, provided that in the best medical judgment of the physician, made at the time of the study, said procedures do not substantially jeopardize the life or health of the fetus, and provided said fetus is not the subject of a planned abortion. In any criminal proceeding the fetus shall be conclusively presumed not to be the subject of a planned abortion if the mother signed a written statement at the time of study, that she was not planning an abortion.

This section shall not prohibit or regulate diagnostic or remedial procedures the purpose of which is to determine the life or health of the fetus involved or to preserve the life or health of the fetus involved or the mother involved.

A fetus is a live fetus for purposes of this section when, in the best medical judgment of a physician, it shows evidence of life as determined by the same medical standards as are used in determining evidence of life in a spontaneously aborted fetus at approximately the same stage of gestational development.

No experimentation may knowingly be performed upon a dead fetus unless the consent of the mother has first been obtained, provided however that such consent shall not be required in the case of a routine pathological study. In any criminal proceeding, consent shall be conclusively presumed to have been granted for the purposes of this section by a written statement, signed by the mother who is at least eighteen years of age, to the effect that she consents to the use of her fetus for scientific, laboratory, research or other kind of experimentation or study; such written consent shall constitute lawful authorization for the transfer of the dead fetus.

No person shall perform or offer to perform an abortion where part or all of the consideration for said performance is that the fetal remains may be used for experimentation or other kind of research or study.

No person shall knowingly sell, transfer, distribute or give away any fetus for a use which is in violation of the provisions of this section. For purposes of this section, the word "fetus" shall include an embryo or neonate.

Whoever violates the provisions of this section shall be punished by imprisonment in a jail or house of correction for not less than one year nor more than two and one half years or by imprisonment in the state prison for not more than five years.

Appendix E

UNIFORM ANATOMICAL GIFT ACT

An Act authorizing the gift of all or part of a human body after death for specified purposes.

SECTION 1. (Definitions.)

(a) "Bank or storage facility" means a facility licensed, accredited, or approved under the laws of any State for storage of human bodies or parts thereof.

(b) "Decedent" means a deceased individual and includes a stillborn infant or fetus.

(c) "Donor" means an individual who makes a gift of all or part of his body.

(d) "Hospital" means a hospital licensed, accredited, or approved under the laws of any State; includes a hospital operated by the United States government, a State, or a subdivision thereof, although not required to be licensed under State laws.

(e) "Part" means organs, tissues, eyes, bones, arteries, blood, other fluids and any other portions of a human body.

(f) "Person" means an individual, corporation, government or governmental subdivision or agency, business trust, estate, trust, partnership or association, or any other legal entity.

(g) "Physician" or "surgeon" means a physician or surgeon licensed or authorized to practice under the laws of any State.

(h) "State" includes any State, district, commonwealth, territory, insular possession, and any other area subject to the legislative authority of the United States of America.

SECTION 2. (Persons Who May Execute an Anatomical Gift.)

(a) Any individual of sound mind and 18 years of age or more may give all or any part of his body for any purpose specified in Section 3, the gift to take effect upon death.

(b) Any of the following persons, in order of priority stated, when persons in prior classes are not available at the time of death, and in the absence of actual notice of contrary indications by the decedent or actual notice of opposition by a member of the same or a prior class, may give all or any part of the decedent's body for any purpose specified in Section 3:

    (1) the spouse,

    (2) an adult son or daughter,

    (3) either parent,

(4) an adult brother or sister,

(5) a guardian of the person of the decedent at the time of his death,

(6) any other person authorized or under obligation to dispose of the body.

(c) If the donee has actual notice of contrary indications by the decedent or that a gift by a member of a class is opposed by a member of the same or a prior class, the donee shall not accept the gift. The persons authorized by subsection (b) may make the gift after or immediately before death.

(d) A gift of all or part of a body authorizes any examination necessary to assure medical acceptability of the gift for the purposes intended.

(e) The rights of the donee created by the gift are paramount to the rights of others except as provided by Section 7 (d).

SECTION 3. (Persons Who May Become Donees; Purposes for Which Anatomical Gifts May be Made.) The following persons may become donees of gifts of bodies or parts thereof for the purposes stated:

(1) any hospital, surgeon, or physician, for medical or dental education, research, advancement of medical or dental science, therapy, or transplantation; or

(2) any accredited medical or dental school, college or university for education, research, advancement of medical or dental science, or therapy; or

(3) any bank or storage facility, for medical or dental education, research, advancement of medical or dental science, therapy, or transplantation; or

(4) any specified individual for therapy or transplantation needed by him.

SECTION 4. (Manner of Executing Anatomical Gifts.)

(a) A gift of all or part of the body under Section 2 (a) may be made by will. The gift becomes effective upon the death of the testator without waiting for probate. If the will is not probated, or if it is declared invalid for testamentary purposes, the gift, to the extent that it has been acted upon in good faith, is nevertheless valid and effective.

(b) A gift of all or part of the body under Section 2 (a) may also be made by document other than a will. The gift becomes effective upon the death of the donor. The document, which may be a card designed to be carried on the person, must be signed by the donor in the presence of 2 witnesses who must sign the document in his presence. If the donor cannot sign, the document may be signed for him at his direction and in his presence in the presence of 2 witnesses who must sign the document in his presence. Delivery of the document of gift during the donor's lifetime is not necessary to make the gift valid.

(c) The gift may be made to a specified donee or without specifying a donee. If the latter, the gift may be accepted by the attending physician as donee upon or following death. If the gift is made to a specified donee who is not available at the time and place of death, the attending physician upon or following death, in the absence of any expressed indication that the donor desired otherwise, may accept the gift as donee. The physician who becomes a donee under this subsection shall not participate in the procedures for removing or transplanting a part.

(d) Notwithstanding Section 7 (b), the donor may designate in his will, card, or other document of gift the surgeon or physician to carry out the appropriate procedures. In the absence of a designation or if the designee is not available, the donee or other person authorized to accept the gift may employ or authorize any surgeon or physician for the purpose.

(e) Any gift by a person designated in Section 2 (b) shall be made by a document signed by him or made by his telegraphic, recorded telephonic, or other recorded message.

SECTION 5. (Delivery of Document of Gift.) If the gift is made by the donor to a specified donee, the will, card, or other document, or an executed copy thereof, may be delivered to the donee to expedite the appropriate procedures immediately after death. Delivery is not necessary to the validity of the gift. The will, card, or other document, or an executed copy thereof, may be deposited in any hospital, bank or storage facility, or registry office that accepts it for safekeeping or for facilitation of procedures after death. On request of any interested party upon or after the donor's death, the person in possession shall produce the document for examination.

SECTION 6. (Amendment or Revocation of the Gift.)

(a) If the will, card, or other document or executed copy thereof, has been delivered to a specified donee, the donor may amend or revoke the gift by:

(1) the execution and delivery to the donee of a signed statement, or

(2) an oral statement made in the presence of 2 persons and communicated to the donee, or

(3) a statement during a terminal illness or injury addressed to an attending physician and communicated to the donee, or

(4) a signed card or document found on his person or in his effects.

(b) Any document of gift which has not been delivered to the donee may be revoked by the donor in the manner set out in subsection (a) or by destruction, cancellation, or mutiliation of the document and all executed copies thereof.

(c) Any gift made by a will may also be amended or revoked in the manner provided for amendment or revocation of wills or as provided in subsection (a).

SECTION 7. (Rights and Duties at Death.)

(a) The donee may accept or reject the gift. If the donee accepts a gift of the entire body, he may, subject to the terms of the gift, authorize embalming and the use of the body in funeral services. If the gift is of a part of the body, the donee, upon the death of the donor and prior to embalming, shall cause the part to be removed without unnecessary mutiliation. After removal of the part, custody of the remainder of the body vests in the surviving spouse, next of kin, or other persons under obligation to dispose of the body.

(b) The time of death shall be determined by a physician who attends the donor at his death, or, if none, the physician who certifies the death. The physician shall not participate in the procedures for removing or transplanting a part.

(c) A person who acts in good faith in accord with the terms of this Act or the anatomical gift laws of another State (or a foreign country) is not liable for damages in any civil action or subject to prosecution in any criminal proceeding for his act.

(d) The provisions of this Act are subject to the laws of this State prescribing powers and duties with respect to autopsies.

SECTION 8. (Uniformity of Interpretation.) This Act shall be so construed as to effectuate its general purpose to make unifrom the law of those States which enact it.

SECTION 9. (Short Title.) This Act may be cited as the Uniform Anatomical Gift Act.

SECTION 10. (Repeal.) The following Acts and parts of Acts are repealed:

(1)

(2)

(3)

SECTION 11. (Time of Taking Effect.) This Act shall take effect

Appendix F

UNIFORM DONOR CARD

UNIFORM DONOR CARD

OF _____
   Print or type name of donor

In the hope that I may help others, I hereby make this anatomical gift, if medically acceptable, to take effect on my death. The words and marks below indicate my desires.

I give: (a) _____ any needed organs or parts
         (b) _____ only the following organs or parts

_____
                Specify the organ(s) or part(s)

for the purposes of transplantation, therapy, medical research or education;

         (c) _____ my body for anatomical study if needed.

Limitations or
special wishes, if any: _____

Signed by the donor and the following two witnesses in the presence of each other:

_____   _____
   Signature of Donor   Date of Birth of Donor

_____   _____
       Date Signed   City & State

_____   _____
         Witness   Witness

This is a legal document under the Uniform Anatomical Gift Act or similar laws.

Appendix G

NATIONAL RESEARCH SERVICE AWARD ACT OF 1974

PUBLIC LAW 93-348; 88 STAT. 342
(H. R. 7724)

Be it enacted by the Senate and House of Representatives of the
United States of America in Congress assembled,
Section 1. This Act may be cited as the "National Research Act".

TITLE I--BIOMEDICAL AND BEHAVIORAL RESEARCH TRAINING

SHORT TITLE

Sec. 101. This title may be cited as the "National Research Service Award Act of 1974".

FINDINGS AND DECLARATION OF PURPOSE

Sec. 102. (a) Congress finds and declares that--

(1) the success and continued viability of the Federal biomedical and behavioral research effort depends on the availability of excellent scientists and a network of institutions of excellence capable of producing superior research personnel;

(2) direct support of the training of scientists for careers in biomedical and behavioral research is an appropriate and necessary role for the Federal Government; and

(3) graduate research assistance programs should be the key elements in the training programs of the institutes of the National Institutes of Health and the Alcohol, Drug Abuse, and Mental Health Administration.

(b) It is the purpose of this title to increase the capability of the institutes of the National Institutes of Health and the Alcohol, Drug Abuse, and Mental Health Administration to carry out their responsibility of maintaining a superior national program of research into the physical and mental diseases and impairments of man.

BIOMEDICAL AND BEHAVIORAL RESEARCH TRAINING

Sec. 103. The part H of the Public Health Service Act relating to the appointment of the Directors of the National Institutes of Health and the National Cancer Institute is redesignated as part I, section 461 of such part is redesignated as section 471, and such part is amended by adding at the end the following new sections:

"NATIONAL RESEARCH SERVICE AWARDS

"Sec. 472. (a) (1) The Secretary shall--

"(A) provide National Research Service Awards for--

"(i) biomedical and behavioral research at the National Institutes of Health and the Alcohol, Drug Abuse, and Mental Health Administration in matters relating to the cause, diagnosis, prevention, and treatment of the disease (or diseases) or other health problems to which the activities of the Institutes and Administration are directed.

"(ii) training at the Institutes and Administration of individuals to undertake such research,

"(iii) biomedical and behavioral research at non-Federal public institutions and at nonprofit private institutions, and

"(iv) pre- and postdoctoral training at such public and private institutions of individuals to undertake such research; and

"(B) make grants to non-Federal public institutions and to nonprofit private institutions to enable such institutions to make to individuals selected by them National Research Service Awards for research (and training to undertake such research) in the matters described in subparagraph (A) (i).
A reference in this subsection to the National Institutes of Health or the Alcohol, Drug Abuse, and Mental Health Administration shall be considered to include the institutes, divisions, and bureaus included in the Institutes or under the Administration, as the case may be.

"(2) National Research Service Awards may not be used to support residencies.

"(3) Effective July 1,1975, National Research Service Awards may be made for research or research training in only those subject areas for which, as determined under section 473, there is a need for personnel.

"(b) (1) No National Research Service Award may be made by the Secretary to any individual unless--

"(A) the individual has submitted to the Secretary an application therefor and the Secretary has approved the application;

"(B) the individual provides, in such form and manner as the Secretary shall by regulation prescribe, assurances satisfactory to the Secretary that the individual will meet the service requirement of subsection (c) (1); and

"(C) in the case of a National Research Service Award for a purpose described in subsection (a) (1) (A) (iii) or (a) (1) (A) (iv), the individual has been sponsored (in such manner as the Secretary may by regulation require) by the institution at which the research or training under the Award will be conducted.

An application for an Award shall be in such form, submitted in such manner, and contain such information, as the Secretary may by regulation prescribe.

"(2) The award of National Research Service Awards by the Secretary under subsection (a) and the making of grants for such Awards shall be subject to review and approval by the appropriate advisory councils to the entities of the National Institutes of Health and the Alcohol, Drug Abuse, and Mental Health Administration (A) whose activities relate to the research or training under the Awards, or (B) at which such research or training will be conducted.

"(3) No grant may be made under subsection (a) (1) (B) unless an application therefor has been submitted to and approved by the Secretary. Such application shall be in such form, submitted in such manner, and contain such information, as the Secretary may by regulation prescribe. Subject to the provisions of this section other than paragraph (1) of this subsection, National Research Service Awards made under a grant under subsection (a) (1) (B) shall be made in accordance with such regulations as the Secretary shall prescribe.

"(4) The period of any National Research Service Award made to any individual under subsection (a) may not exceed three years in the aggregate unless the Secretary for good cause shown waives the application of the three-year limit to such individual.

"(5) National Research Service Awards shall provide for such stipends and allowances (including travel and subsistence expenses and dependency allowances) for the recipients of the Awards as the Secretary may deem necessary. A National Research Service Award made to an individual for research or research training at a non-Federal public or nonprofit private institution shall also provide for payments to be made to the institution for the cost of support services (including the cost of faculty salaries, supplies, equipment, general research support, and related items) provided such individual by such institution. The amount of any such payments to any institution shall be determined by the Secretary and shall bear a direct relationship to the reasonable costs of the institution for establishing and maintaining the quality of its biomedical and behavioral research and training programs.

"(c) (1) (A) Each individual who receives a National Research Service Award shall, in accordance with paragraph (3), engage in--

"(i) health research or teaching,

"(ii) if authorized under subparagraph (B), serve as a member of the National Health Service Corps or serve in his specialty, or

"(iii) if authorized under subparagraph (C), serve in a health related activity approved under that subparagraph,

for a period computed in accordance with paragraph (2).

"(B) Any individual who received a National Research Service Award and who is a physician, dentist, nurse, or other individual trained to provide health care directly to individual patients may, upon application to the Secretary, be authorized by the Secretary to--

"(i) serve as a member of the National Health Service Corps,

"(ii) serve in his specialty in private practice in a geographic area designated by the Secretary as requiring that specialty, or

"(iii) provide services in his specialty for a health maintenance organization to which payments may be made under section 1876 of title XVIII of the Social Security Act and which serves a medically underserved population (as defined in section 1302(7) of this Act),

in lieu of engaging in health research or teaching if the Secretary determines that there are no suitable health research or teaching positions available to such individual.

"(C) Where appropriate the Secretary may, upon application, authorize a recipient of a National Research Service Award, who is not trained to provide health care directly to individual patients, to engage in a health-related activity in lieu of engaging in health research or teaching if the Secretary determines that there are no suitable health research or teaching positions available to such individual.

"(2) For each year for which an individual receives a National Research Service Award he shall--

"(A) for twelve months engage in health research or teaching or, if so authorized, serve as a member of the National Health Service Corps, or

"(B) if authorized under paragraph (1) (B) or (1) (C), for twenty months serve in his specialty or engage in a health-related activity.

"(3) The requirement of paragraph (1) shall be complied with by any individual to whom it applies within such reasonable period of time, after the completion of such individual's Award, as the Secretary shall by regulation prescribe. The Secretary shall (A) by regulation prescribe (i) the type of research and teaching which an individual may engage in to comply with such requirement, and (ii) such other requirements respecting such research and teaching and alternative service authorized under paragraphs (1) (B) and (1) (C) as he deems necessary; and (B) to the extent feasible, provide that the members of the National Health Service Corps who are serving in the Corps to meet the requirement of paragraph (1) shall be assigned to patient care and to positions which utilize the clinical training and experience of the members.

"(4) (A) If any individual to whom the requirement of paragraph (1) is applicable fails, within the period prescribed by paragraph (3), to comply with such requirement, the United States shall be entitled to recover from such individual an amount determined in accordance with the formula--

$$A = \phi \left(\frac{t - 1/2s}{t} \right)$$

in which 'A' is the amount the United States is entitled to recover; 'ϕ' is the sum of the total amount paid under one or more National Research Service Awards to such individual and the interest on such amount would be payable if at the time it was paid it was a loan bearing interest at a rate fixed by the Secretary of the Treasury after taking into consideration private consumer rates of interest prevailing at the time each Award to such individual was made; 't' is the total number of months in such individual's service obligation; and 's' is the number of months of such obligation served by him in accordance with paragraphs (1) and (2) of this subsection.

"(B) Any amount which the United States is entitled to recover under subparagraph (A) shall, within the three-year period beginning on the date the United States becomes entitled to recover such amount, be paid to the United States. Until any amount due the United States under subparagraph (A) on account of any National Research Service Award is paid, there shall accrue to the United States interest on such amount at the same rate as that fixed by the Secretary of the Treasury under subparagraph (A) to determine the amount due the United States.

"(4) (A) Any obligation of any individual under paragraph (3) shall be canceled upon the death of such individual.

"(B) The Secretary shall by regulation provide for the waiver or suspension of any such obligation applicable to any individual whenever compliance by such individual is impossible or would involve extreme hardship to such individual and if enforcement of such obligation with respect to any individual would be against equity and good conscience.

"(d) There are authorized to be appropriated to make payments under National Research Service Awards and under grants for such Awards $207,947,000 for the fiscal year ending June 30, 1975. Of the sums appropriated under this subsection, not less than 25 per centum shall be made available for payments under National Research Service Awards provided by the Secretary under subsection (a) (1) (A).

"STUDIES RESPECTING BIOMEDICAL AND BEHAVIORAL RESEARCH PERSONNEL

"Sec. 473. (a) The Secretary shall, in accordance with subsection (b), arrange for the conduct of a continuing study to--

"(1) establish (A) the Nation's overall need for biomedical and behavioral research personnel, (B) the subject areas in which such personnel are needed and the number of such personnel needed in each such area, and (C) the kinds and extent of training which should be provided such personnel;

"(2) assess (A) current training programs available for the training of biomedical and behavioral research personnel which are conducted under this Act at or through institutes under the National Institutes of Health and the Alcohol, Drug Abuse, and Mental Health Administration, and (B) other current training programs available for the training of such personnel;

"(3) identify the kinds of research positions available to and held by individuals completing such programs;

"(4) determine, to the extent feasible, whether the programs referred to in clause (B) of paragraph (2) would be adequate to meet the needs established under paragraph (1) if the programs referred to in clause (A) of paragraph (2) were terminated; and

"(5) determine what modifications in the programs referred to in paragraph (2) are required to meet the needs established under paragraph (1).

"(b) (1) The Secretary shall request the National Academy of

Sciences to conduct the study required by subsection (a) under an arrangement under which the actual expenses incurred by such Academy in conducting such study will be paid by the Secretary. If the National Academy of Sciences is willing to do so, the Secretary shall enter into such an arrangement with such Academy for the conduct of such study.

"(2) If the National Academy of Sciences is unwilling to conduct such study under such an arrangement, then the Secretary shall enter into a similar arrangement with other appropriate nonprofit private groups or associations under which such groups or associations will conduct such study and prepare and submit the reports thereon as provided in subsection (c).

"(c) A report on the results of such study shall be submitted by the Secretary to the Committee on Interstate and Foreign Commerce of the House of Representatives and the Committee on Labor and Public Welfare of the Senate not later than March 31 of each year."

CONFORMING AMENDMENTS

Sec. 104. (a) (1) Section 301 of the Public Health Service Act is amended (A) by striking out paragraph (c); (B) by striking out in paragraph (d) "or research training" each place it occurs, "and research training programs", and "and research training program"; and (C) by redesignating paragraphs (d), (e), (f), (g), (h), and (i) as paragraphs (c), (d), (e), (f), (g), and (h), respectively.

(2) (A) Section 303(a) (1) of such Act is amended to read as follows:

"(1) to provide clinical training and instruction and to establish and maintain clinical traineeships (with such stipends and allowances (including travel and subsistence expenses and dependency allowances) for the trainees as the Secretary may deem necessary);".

(B) Section 303(b) of such Act is amended by inserting before the first sentence the following: "The Secretary may provide for training, instruction, and traineeships under subsection (a) (1) through grants to public and other nonprofit institutions.".

(3) Section 402(a) of such Act is amended (A) by striking out "training and instruction" in paragraph (3) and inserting in lieu thereof "clinical training and instruction", and (B) by striking out paragraph (4) and by redesignating paragraphs (5), (6), and (7) as paragraphs (4), (5), and (6), respectively.

(4) Section 407(b) (7) of such Act is amended (A) by striking out "and basic research and treatment", and (B) by striking out "where appropriate".

(5) Section 408(b)(3) of such Act is amended by inserting "clinical" before "training" each place it occurs.

(6) Section 412(7) of such Act is amended by striking out "(1) establish and maintain" and all that follows down through and including "maintain traineeships" and inserting in lieu thereof ", provide clinical training and instruction and establish and maintain clinical traineeships".

(7) Section 413(a)(7) is amended by inserting "clinical" before "programs".

(8) Section 415(b) is amended by inserting before the period at the end of the last sentence thereof the following: "; and the term 'training' does not include research training for which fellowship support may be provided under section 472".

(9) Section 422 of such Act is amended (A) by striking out paragraph (c) and by redesignating paragraphs (d), (e), and (f) as paragraphs (c), (d), and (e), respectively, and (B) by striking out "training and instruction and establish and maintain traineeships" in paragraph (e) (as so redesignated) and inserting in lieu thereof "clinical training and instruction and establish and maintain clinical traineeships".

(10) Section 434(c)(2) of such Act is amended by inserting "(other than research training for which National Research Service Awards may be made under section 472)" after "training" the first time it occurs.

(11) Sections 433(a), 444, and 453 of such Act are each amended by striking out the second sentence thereof.

(12) The heading for part I of title IV of such Act (as so redesignated by section 103) is amended by striking out "Administrative" and inserting in lieu thereof "General."

(b) The amendments made by subsection (a) shall not apply with respect to commitments made before the date of the enactment of this Act by the Secretary of Health, Education, and Welfare for research training under the provisions of the Public Health Service Act amended or repealed by subsection (a).

SEX DISCRIMINATION

Sec. 105. Section 799A of the Public Health Service Act is amended by adding at the end thereof the following: "In the case of a school of medicine which--

"(1) on the date of the enactment of this sentence is in the process of changing its status as an institution which admits only female students to that of an institution which admits students without regard to their sex, and

"(2) is carrying out such change in accordance with a plan approved by the Secretary,

the provisions of the preceding sentences of this section shall apply only with respect to a grant, contract, loan guarantee, or interest subsidy to, or for the benefit of such a school for a fiscal year beginning after June 30, 1979."

FINANCIAL DISTRESS GRANTS

Sec. 106. Section 773(a) of the Public Health Service Act is amended (1) by striking out "$10,000,000" and inserting in lieu thereof "$15,000,000", and (2) by striking out "1972" each place it occurs in the last sentence thereof and inserting in lieu thereof "1974".

TITLE II--PROTECTION OF HUMAN SUBJECTS OF BIOMEDICAL AND BEHAVIORAL RESEARCH

PART A--NATIONAL COMMISSION FOR THE PROTECTION OF HUMAN SUBJECTS OF BIOMEDICAL AND BEHAVIORAL RESEARCH

ESTABLISHMENT OF COMMISSION

Sec. 201. (a) There is established a Commission to be known as the National Commission for the Protection of Human Subjects of Biomedical and Behavioral Research (hereinafter in this title referred to as the "Commission").

(b) (1) The Commission shall be composed of eleven members appointed by the Secretary of Health, Education, and Welfare (hereinafter in this title referred to as the "Secretary"). The Secretary shall select members of the Commission from individuals distinguished in the fields of medicine, law, ethics, theology, the biological, physical, behavioral and social sciences, philosophy, humanities, health administration, government, and public affairs; but five (and not more than five) of the members of the Commission shall be individuals who are or who have been engaged in biomedical or behavioral research involving human subjects. In appointing members of the Commission, the Secretary shall give consideration to recommendations from the National Academy of Sciences and other appropriate entities. Members of the Commission shall be appointed for the life of the Commission. The Secretary shall appoint the members of the Commission within sixty days of the date of the enactment of this Act.

(2) (A) Except as provided in subparagraph (B), members of

the Commission shall each be entitled to receive the daily equivalent of the annual rate of the basic pay in effect for grade GS-18 of the General Schedule for each day (including traveltime) during which they are engaged in the actual performance of the duties of the Commission.

(B) Members of the Commission who are full-time officers or employees of the United States shall receive no additional pay on account of their service on the Commission.

(C) While away from their homes or regular places of business in the performance of duties of the Commission, members of the Commission shall be allowed travel expenses, including per diem in lieu of subsistence, in the same manner as persons employed intermittently in the Government service are allowed expenses under section 5703(b) of title 5 of the United States Code.

(c) The chairman of the Commission shall be selected by the members of the Commission from among their number.

(d) (1) The Commission may appoint and fix the pay of such staff personnel as it deems desirable. Such personnel shall be appointed subject to the provisions of title 5, United States Code, governing appointments in the competitive service, and shall be paid in accordance with the provisions of chapter 51 and subchapter III of chapter 53 of such title relating to classification and General Schedule pay rates.

(2) The Commission may procure temporary and intermittent services to the same extent as is authorized by section 3109(b) of title 5 of the United States Code, but at rates for individuals not to exceed the daily equivalent of the annual rate of basic pay in effect for grade GS-18 of the General Schedule.

COMMISSION DUTIES

Sec. 202. (a) The Commission shall carry out the following:

(1) (A) The Commission shall (i) conduct a comprehensive investigation and study to identify the basic ethical principles which should underlie the conduct of biomedical and behavioral research involving human subjects, (ii) develop guidelines which should be followed in such research to assure that it is conducted in accordance with such principles, and (iii) make recommendations to the Secretary (I) for such administrative action as may be appropriate to apply such guidelines to biomedical and behavioral research conducted or supported under programs administered by the Secretary, and (II) concerning any other matter pertaining to the protection of human subjects of biomedical and behavioral research.

(B) In carrying out subparagraph (A), the Commission shall consider at least the following:

(i) The boundaries between biomedical or behavioral research involving human subjects and the accepted and routine practice of medicine.

(ii) The role of assessment of risk-benefit criteria in the determination of the appropriateness of research involving human subjects.

(iii) Appropriate guidelines for the selection of human subjects for participation in biomedical and behavioral research.

(iv) The nature and definition of informed consent in various research settings.

(v) Mechanisms for evaluating and monitoring the performance of Institutional Review Boards established in accordance with section 474 of the Public Health Service Act and appropriate enforcement mechanisms for carrying out their decisions.

(C) The Commission shall consider the appropriateness of applying the principles and guidelines identified and developed under subparagraph (A) to the delivery of health services to patients under programs conducted or supported by the Secretary.

(2) The Commission shall identify the requirements for informed consent to participation in biomedical and behavioral research by children, prisoners, and the institutionalized mentally infirm. The Commission shall investigate and study biomedical and behavioral research conducted or supported under programs administered by the Secretary and involving children, prisoners, and the institutionalized mentally infirm to determine the nature of the consent obtained from such persons or their legal representatives before such persons were involved in such research; the adequacy of the information given them respecting the nature and purpose of the research, procedures to be used, risks and discomforts, anticipated benefits from the research, and other matters necessary for informed consent; and the competence and the freedom of the persons to make a choice for or against involvement in such research. On the basis of such investigation and study the Commission shall make such recommendations to the Secretary as it determines appropriate to assure that biomedical and behavioral research conducted or supported under programs administered by him meets the requirements respecting informed consent identified by the Commission. For purposes of this paragraph, the term "children" means individuals who have not attained the legal age of consent to participate in research as determined under the applicable law of the jurisdiction in which the research is to be conducted; the term

"prisoner" means individuals involuntarily confined in correctional institutions or facilities (as defined in section 601 of the Omnibus Crime Control and Safe Streets Act of 1968 (42 U.S.C. 3781)); and the term "institutionalized mentally infirm" includes individuals who are mentally ill, mentally retarded, emotionally disturbed, psychotic, or senile, or who have other impairments of a similar nature and who reside as patients in an institution.

(3) The Commission shall conduct an investigation and study to determine the need for a mechanism to assure that human subjects in biomedical and behavioral research not subject to regulation by the Secretary are protected. If the Commission determines that such a mechanism is needed, it shall develop and recommend to the Congress such a mechanism. The Commission may contract for the design of such a mechanism to be included in such recommendations.

(b) The Commission shall conduct an investigation and study of the nature and extent of research involving living fetuses, the purposes for which such research has been undertaken, and alternative means for achieving such purposes. The Commission shall, not later than the expiration of the 4-month period beginning on the first day of the first month that follows the date on which all the members of the Commission have taken office, recommend to the Secretary policies defining the circumstances (if any) under which such research may be conducted or supported.

(c) The Commission shall conduct an investigation and study of the use of psychosurgery in the United States during the five-year period ending December 31, 1972. The Commission shall determine the appropriateness of its use, evaluate the need for it, and recommend to the Secretary policies defining the circumstances (if any) under which its use may be appropriate. For purposes of this paragraph, the term "psychosurgery" means brain surgery on (1) normal brain tissue of an individual, who does not suffer from any physical disease, for the purpose of changing or controlling the behavior or emotions of such individual, or (2) diseased brain tissue of an individual, if the sole object of the performance of such surgery is to control, change, or affect any behavioral or emotional disturbance of such individual. Such term does not include brain surgery designed to cure or ameliorate the effects of epilepsy and electric shock treatments.

(d) The Commission shall make recommendations to the Congress respecting the functions and authority of the National Advisory Council for the Protection of Subjects of Biomedical and Behavioral Research to be established under section 217(f) of the Public Health Service Act.

SPECIAL STUDY

Sec. 203. The Commission shall undertake a comprehensive study of the ethical, social, and legal implications of advances in biomedical and behavioral research and technology. Such study shall include--

(1) an analysis and evaluation of scientific and technological advances in past, present, and projected biomedical and behavioral research and services;

(2) an analysis and evaluation of the implications of such advances, both for individuals and for society;

(3) an analysis and evaluation of laws and moral and ethical principles governing the use of technology in medical practice;

(4) an analysis and evaluation of public understanding of and attitudes toward such implications and laws and principles; and

(5) an analysis and evaluation of implications for public policy of such findings as are made by the Commission with respect to advances in biomedical and behavioral research and technology and public attitudes toward such advances.

ADMINISTRATIVE PROVISIONS

Sec. 204. (a) The Commission may for the purpose of carrying out its duties under sections 202 and 203 hold such hearings, sit and act at such times and places, take such testimony, and receive such evidence as the Commission deems advisable.

(b) The Commission may secure directly from any department or agency of the United States information necessary to enable it to carry out its duties. Upon the request of the chairman of the Commission, the head of such department or agency shall furnish such information to the Commission.

(c) The Commission shall not disclose any information reported to or otherwise obtained by it in carrying out its duties which (1) identifies any individual who has been the subject of an activity studied and investigated by the Commission, or (2) which concerns any information which contains or relates to a trade secret or other matter referred to in section 1905 of title 18 of the United States Code.

(d) Except as provided in subsection (b) of section 202, the Commission shall complete its duties under sections 202 and 203 not later than the expiration of the 24-month period beginning on the first day of the first month that follows the date on which all the members of the Commission have taken office. The Commission shall make periodic reports to the President, the Congress, and the Secretary respecting its activities under sections 202 and

203 shall, not later than ninety days after the expiration of such 24-month period, make a final report to the President, the Congress, and the Secretary respecting such activities and including its recommendations for administrative action and legislation.

(e) The Commission shall cease to exist thirty days following the submission of its final report pursuant to subsection (d).

DUTIES OF THE SECRETARY

Sec. 205. Within 60 days of the receipt of any recommendation made by the Commission under section 202, the Secretary shall publish it in the Federal Register and provide opportunity for interested persons to submit written data, views, and arguments with respect to such recommendation. The Secretary shall consider the Commission's recommendation and relevant matter submitted with respect to it and, within 180 days of the date of its publication in the Federal Register, the Secretary shall (1) determine whether the administrative action proposed by such recommendation is appropriate to assure the protection of human subjects of biomedical and behavioral research conducted or supported under programs administered by him, and (2) if he determines that such action is not so appropriate, publish in the Federal Register such determination together with an adequate statement of the reasons for his determination. If the Secretary determines that administrative action recommended by the Commission should be undertaken by him, he shall undertake such action as expeditiously as is feasible.

PART B--MISCELLANEOUS

NATIONAL ADVISORY COUNCIL FOR THE PROTECTION OF SUBJECTS OF BIOMEDICAL AND BEHAVIORAL RESEARCH

Sec. 211. (a) Section 217 of the Public Health Service Act is amended by adding at the end the following new subsection:

"(f) (1) There shall be established a National Advisory Council for the Protection of Subjects of Biomedical and Behavioral Research (hereinafter in this subsection referred to as the 'Council') which shall consist of the Secretary who shall be Chairman and not less than seven nor more than fifteen other members who shall be appointed by the Secretary without regard to the provisions of title 5, United States Code, governing appointments in the competitive service. The Secretary shall select members of the Council from individuals distinguished in the fields of medicine, law, ethics, theology, the biological, physical, behavioral and social sciences, philosophy, humanities, health administration, government, and public affairs; but three (and not more than three) of the members of the Council shall be individuals who are or who have been engaged in biomedical or behavioral research involving human subjects. No individual who was appointed to be a member of the National Commission for the Protection of Human Subjects of Biomedical and Behavioral Research (established under title II of the National Research Act) may be appointed to be a member of the Council. The appointed members of the Council shall have terms of office of four years, except that for the purpose of staggering the expiration of the terms of office of the Council members, the Secretary shall, at the time of appointment, designate a term of office of less than four years for members first appointed to the Council.

"(2) The Council shall--

"(A) advise, consult with, and make recommendations to, the Secretary concerning all matters pertaining to the protection of human subjects of biomedical and behavioral research;

"(B) review policies, regulations, and other requirements of the Secretary governing such research to determine the extent to which such policies, regulations, and requirements require and are effective in requiring observance in such research of the basic ethical principles which should underlie the conduct of such research and, to the extent such policies, regulations, or requirements do not require or are not effective in requiring observance of such principles, make recommendations to the Secretary respecting appropriate revision of such policies, regulations, or requirements; and

"(C) review periodically changes in the scope, purpose, and types of biomedical and behavioral research being conducted and the impact such changes have on the policies, regulations, and other requirements of the Secretary for the protection of human subjects of such research.

"(3) The Council may disseminate to the public such information, recommendations, and other matters relating to its functions as it deems appropriate.

"(4) Section 14 of the Federal Advisory Committee Act shall not apply with respect to the Council."

(b) The amendment made by subsection (a) shall take effect July 1, 1976.

INSTITUTIONAL REVIEW BOARDS; ETHICS GUIDANCE PROGRAM

Sec. 212. (a) Part I of title IV of the Public Health Service Act, as amended by section 103 of this Act, is amended by adding at the end the following new section:

"INSTITUTIONAL REVIEW BOARDS; ETHICS GUIDANCE PROGRAM

"Sec. 474. (a) The Secretary shall by regulation require that each entity which applies for a grant or contract under this Act for any project or program which involves the conduct of biomedical or behavioral research involving human subjects submit in or with its application for such grant or contract assurances satisfactory to the Secretary that it has established (in accordance with regulations which the Secretary shall prescribe) a board (to be known as an 'Institutional Review Board') to review biomedical and behavioral research involving human subjects conducted at or sponsored by such entity in order to protect the rights of the human subjects of such research.

"(b) The Secretary shall establish a program within the Department under which requests for clarification and guidance with respect to ethical issues raised in connection with biomedical or behavioral research involving human subjects are responded to promptly and appropriately."

(b) The Secretary of Health, Education, and Welfare shall within 240 days of the date of the enactment of this Act promulgate such regulations as may be required to carry out section 474(a) of the Public Health Service Act. Such regulations shall apply with respect to applications for grants and contracts under such Act submitted after promulgation of such regulations.

LIMITATION ON RESEARCH

Sec. 213. Until the Commission has made its recommendations to the Secretary pursuant to section 202(b), the Secretary may not conduct or support research in the United States or abroad on a living human fetus, before or after the induced abortion of such fetus, unless such research is done for the purpose of assuring the survival of such fetus.

INDIVIDUAL RIGHTS

Sec. 214. (a) Subsection (c) of section 401 of the Health Programs Extension Act of 1973 is amended (1) by inserting "(1)" after "(c)", (2) by redesignating paragraphs (1) and (2) as subparagraphs (A) and (B), respectively, and (3) by adding at the end the following new paragraph:

"(2) No entity which receives after the date of enactment of this paragraph a grant or contract for biomedical or behavioral research under any program administered by the Secretary of Health, Education, and Welfare may--

"(A) discriminate in the employment, promotion, or termination of employment of any physician or other health care personnel, or

"(B) discriminate in the extension of staff or other privileges to any physician or other health care personnel,

because he performed or assisted in the performance of any lawful health service or research activity, because he refused to perform or assist in the performance of any such service or activity on the grounds that his performance or assistance in the performance of such service or activity would be contrary to his religious beliefs or moral convictions, or because of his religious beliefs or moral convictions respecting any such service or activity."

(b) Section 401 of such Act is amended by adding at the end the following new subsection:

"(d) No individual shall be required to perform or assist in the performance of any part of a health service program or research activity funded in whole or in part under a program administered by the Secretary of Health, Education, and Welfare if his performance or assistance in the performance of such part of such program or activity would be contrary to his religious beliefs or moral convictions."

SPECIAL PROJECT GRANTS AND CONTRACTS

Sec. 215. Section 772(a)(7) of the Public Health Service Act is amended by inserting immediately before the semicolon at the end thereof the following: ", or (C) providing increased emphasis on the ethical, social, legal, and moral implications of advances in biomedical research and technology with respect to the effects of such advances on individuals and society".

Approved July 12, 1974.

TABLE OF CASES

TABLE OF CASES

Bonner v. Moran (1941), 55

Buck v. Bell (1927), 34-35, 37

Carpenter v. Blake (1872), 18

Cook v. State (1972), 35

Doe v. Bolton (1973), 42

Griswold v. Connecticut (1965), 39, 41-42

Hathaway v. Worcester City Hospital (1973), 41-42

Jacobson v. Massachusetts (1905), 35

Jessin v. County of Shasta (1969), 40-42

Kaimowitz v. Department of Mental Health (1973), 76-77

Mackey v. Procunier (1973), 75

New York City Health and Hospitals Corporation v. Stein (1972), 75

Roe v. Wade (1973), 39-42, 45, 47

Slater v. Baker (1767), 18

Strunk v. Strunk (1969), 56

INDEX

INDEX

Abortion, 39-41, 45-49
Abortion Act, 46
Addicted persons, 9, 13-14
Administrative law, 17, 28-30
Aged persons, 9-10
Assault, 20, 43, 55

Behavior control, 69-70, 76-77
Birth control, 3, 32-44
Breach of contract, 24, 43

Cadaver donors, 52, 54, 56-57
Civil liability, 19, 43, 61, 65-66
Common law, 16-19, 25-26, 28, 30, 43, 46-47, 53, 55, 64
Compulsory sterilization, 33-37
Consent, 9, 14, 21-23, 37, 42, 49, 54-57, 59-61, 73-77
Contract law, 23-25
Criminal liability, 19, 28, 42-43, 61, 65-66

Death, 57-59, 66
Deceit, 43
Department of Health, Education, and Welfare, 48-49
Donors, 47, 51-57, 59-61, 64-66
Drugs, 3, 48, 69-70, 72, 75-76

Environment therapy, 68, 75
Ethics, 6-14

Feeble-minded persons, 9-10, 34
Fetal experimentation, 45-50
Fetus, 40-42, 45-49
Fraud, 20, 43

Group therapy, 68

Incompetents, 54-56, 61, 73
Infant Life (Preservation) Act, 46

Marital relationship, 21, 38, 43
Mayhem, 43
Medical malpractice, 18-19, 60-61, 66
Mental or emotional distress, 21
Mental illness, 9-10, 36, 68-77
Minors, 9, 54-56, 61
Misrepresentation, 25, 43

National Commission for the Protection of Human Subjects of Biomedical and Behavioral Research, 30, 48, 50
National Conference on Uniform Laws, 63-64
National Research Service Award Act, 45, 48
Nazi Germany, 43-44
Negligence, 19-20, 43, 61

Prisoners, 9, 11, 71-75
Privacy, 20-21, 39-41, 71, 76
Psychoanalysis, 68
Psychological experimentation, 68-77
Psychopharmacology, 69-70, 74-75
Psychosurgery, 69-70, 72, 74, 76-77
Psychotherapy, 68-70

Quickening, 46-47

Recipients, 51-52, 54, 56, 59-61, 65-66

Shock therapy, 69-70, 72, 74-75
Socio-economically deprived persons, 9, 11-13, 18, 36, 40
Somatic treatment of mental illness, 68-74, 77
Statutory law, 16, 26-28, 30, 64
Sterilization, 20, 32-44

Test tube babies, 15, 21
Tort Claims Act, 1
Tort law, 19-23
Transplantation, 24, 48, 51-62
Tuskegee Alabama Syphilis Experiment, 1

Uniform Anatomical Gift Act, 54, 57, 59, 63-67
Uniform Donor Card, 65
United States Constitution, 17, 27, 31, 35, 49, 67, 71-73, 76
United States House Committee on Interstate and Foreign Commerce, 15
United States Senate Committee on Labor and Public Welfare, 2, 15, 77

Viability, 40, 47
Voluntary sterilization, 37-42
Volunteers, 11-12